EDMOND ROSTAND

Born in Marseilles in 1868, Rostand wrote in reaction to the prevailing vogue for Naturalism. His first performed play, *Les Romanesques*, was staged by the Comédie-Française in 1894. *La Princesse Lointaine* (1895) provided a leading role for Sarah Bernhardt, as did *La Samaritaine* (1897). Rostand's most famous character, Cyrano de Bergerac, was first created by Coquelin at the Porte-Saint-Martin in 1897 and repeated over four hundred times. There followed *L'Aiglon* (1900) and *Chantecler* (1910), first performed by Lucien Guitry after the death of Coquelin for whom Rostand had written it. *La Derniere Nuit de Don Juan* was left unfinished at Rostand's death in Paris in 1918.

ANTHONY BURGESS

Author of over fifty books, including novels such as *A Clockwork Orange* (1962), *The Malayan Trilogy* (1965), *1985* (1978) and *Earthly Powers* (1980), several critical works and a biography of Shakespeare, Burgess has also written a ballet (*Mr W.S.*), an opera (*The Blooms of Dublin*), several stage plays, film and television scripts, as well as translations such as *Oedipos the King* and *Cyrano*.

Other Titles in this Series

Edmond Rostand

CYRANO DE BERGERAC

translated and adapted by Anthony Burgess

NICK HERN BOOKS

London

www.nickhernbooks.co.uk

A Nick Hern Book

This translation of *Cyrano de Bergerac* first published in this edition in Great Britain in 1991 as a paperback original by Nick Hern Books Limited, The Glasshouse, 49a Goldhawk Road, London W12 8QP

Reprinted 1995, 1999, 2002, 2009, 2013

This translation of *Cyrano de Bergerac* in this edition copyright © 1991 Anthony Burgess

Anthony Burgess has asserted his right to be identified as the author of this translation

First published in Great Britain by Hutchinson & Co. (Publishers) Ltd. in 1985 © Anthony Burgess 1985

Printed in the UK by Mimeo Ltd, Huntingdon, Cambs PE29 6XX

A CIP catalogue record for this book is available from the British Library

ISBN 978 1 85459 117 3

Woodland CARBON
www.woodlandcarbon.co.uk
NICK HERN BOOKS
Printed on Carbon Captured paper

Introduction

This rendering of Rostand's *comédie héroïque en cinq actes en vers* was commissioned for production by the Royal Shakespeare Company at the Barbican Theatre in London in the summer of 1983. But I had previously been commissioned, thirteen years earlier in fact, to translate and adapt the work for the Tyrone Guthrie Theater in Minneapolis, Minnesota, USA. It was proposed that Christopher Plummer play the lead, but the part was taken instead by Paul Hecht. That was in the summer of 1971. The following year a Broadway musical was made out of this version, with lyrics by myself and music by the Welsh film composer Michael Lewis. In this Plummer played the lead – his first and last singing role (I do not think his few *parlando* interjections in *The Sound of Music* can be termed singing). The musical opened at a bad time – the time of the Watergate revelations – and it suffered from union problems. Moreover, though I participated in what amounted to a vulgarization of the original – chiefly in the hope of making money which I did not, in fact, make – I had always had my doubts about the musicalization of *Cyrano de Bergerac*, as it had seemed to me that there was already enough music in the words. I worked too hard on the editing, fresh adaptation and provision of new lyrics (a total of eighty-one, I remember). Perpetually changing *Cyrano*, as the musical was called, to make it more acceptable to a fairly indifferent public, was a daily business, and it was like working on the repair of an aircraft in flight. I was at the time doing a full-time academic job as Distinguished Professor at the City College of New York; I was also helping aspiring writers in a creative writing course; I was also lecturing all over the United States at various universities. It was too much.

The Tyrone Guthrie Theater version (published by Knopf in December 1971 and still in print) was commissioned by the artistic director of the theatre, Michael Langham, and he proposed that the original text be somewhat radically changed. Of all the characters in the play, the least satisfactory to a modern audience appeared to be Roxane (whose name was degallicized to Roxana). She loves Christian, and yet she rebuffs him because he cannot woo her in witty and poetic language. This must seem very improbable in an age that finds a virtue in sincere inarticulacy, and I was told to find an excuse for this near-pathological dismissal of a good wordless soldier whose beauty, on her own admission, fills Roxane's heart with ravishment. So I inserted a little speech which I hoped would ring plausibly, to the effect that inarticulate brutish wooing was a mark of the aristocracy that would regard a middle-class bookish pretty girl like Roxane as fair game, and that to her the advent of true love must reveal itself in divine eloquence. This was meant to add a human substratum to Roxane's preciosity. On the American stage it seemed to work.

But, adding to her lines in Act III, I had to subtract her entire physical presence from Act IV. Her sudden appearance outside the walls of besieged Arras, with gifts of wine, cold chicken and sausage for the starving Gascony cadets, relieved the tension of a scene which, the director insisted, should remain taut to the end, and it was felt that it relieved it in an unworthy manner – through farce and the atmosphere of a fairy tale. Apart from the difficulty of staging (and it is this scene more than anything which puts good amateur companies off the play), everything that is good in this phase of the action seemed to the director to go bad as soon as Roxane came on in her coach and Paris perfume. The hungry cadets cease to be heroic and become merely foppish. They are nearly dying of starvation, and yet they have to go through the motions of taking an elegant little dinner, complete with cutlery and napery. They become mean; they make sure that de Guiche, their detested colonel, who is as ill from hunger as they are, gets nothing of their feast. We may be persuaded, with difficulty, that they now feel fine, but there is a nasty taste in our mouths. Then comes Roxane's avowal to Christian: it is his soul she loves, she tells him, not his physical beauty: she would prefer him to be ugly so that his spiritual qualities may shine the more. All this is on a battlefield, with death ready to arrive at any moment. The whole thing, so Michael Langham believed, became absurd, farcical, unacceptable in terms of even the most far-fetched dramatic convention. He said it had to go, so it went.

I had to substitute for Roxane's personal appearance the arrival of a letter from her, which she, distant and disembodied, had to breathe into a microphone while the lights dimmed and perfume was sprayed through the auditorium. I was amused to find Langham's radical desire for such a change abetted by a Mr Magoo cartoon film, in which Mr Magoo, playing Cyrano, returns amid shells and snipers from mailing the daily letter to Roxane with a letter from the beloved herself in his hand. Roxane's Platonic rhetoric comes off well enough when we can take it as epistolary literature, but, to some, and certainly to Langham, it sounds unreal on speaking lips.

I made, on my own initiative, a less fundamental change in Act III. Roxane and Christian are being hurriedly married by a Capuchin duped into performing the act, and Cyrano has to prevent de Guiche – who wants Roxane as a mistress and has, through his uncle Cardinal Richelieu, power over the entire Capuchin order – from discovering that the ceremony is taking place and stopping it. In the original, Cyrano pretends to have fallen from outer space and he insists on telling de Guiche – who does not see the outsize nose and thinks he is being accosted by a madman – the various possible ways of getting to the moon. Since, at the time of the first production of my version, we had not long been celebrating the moon landing, it seemed that there was a danger that the audience might feel very superior to Cyrano (who, incidentally, as a historical personage wrote the world's first science fiction) and ignore his ingenuity while wanting to put him right on rocketry. So I wrote a couple of speeches in the satirical vein of the historical Cyrano, which could be taken as prefiguring the polemic indiscretion that (in the play, fifteen years later) is the cause of his assassination. It does not greatly matter what Cyrano does to prevent de Guiche's discovery of the clandestine wedding, since it is merely a matter of filling in time entertainingly. Damn it, he could dance and sing, as Christopher Plummer eventually did.

Michael Langham suggested merging the characters of Le Bret and Carbon de Castel-Jaloux to make one meaty personage instead of two thin ones. I did this. I also, at his behest, had the poet Lignière recite some lines from the libellous poem that is the cause of Cyrano's fight with a hundred armed ruffians. It was my own idea to make Cyrano improvise a kind of acrostic on his name in Act II, instead of leaving it to a poet to go home and do it for him. For the rest, the Tyrone Guthrie Theater version was close enough to the play as Rostand wrote it, except for one or two lops of Occam's razor.

The version you have in your hands has many passages in common with that American Ur-adaptation (those two additions just mentioned, for instance), but it represents an almost total return to Rostand's text. A translator-adaptor is a servant of the originating producer or director. Formerly a servant of Michael Langham and of Michael Kidd (for the Broadway musical version), I became a servant of Terry Hands, the director of the Royal Shakespeare Company. He, a French scholar, did not want too many departures from Rostand. He also wanted an English version which should be in neither prose, blank verse nor relentless heroic couplets. In other words, something on the lines of the Tyrone Guthrie Theater version, but without too many fanciful reworkings of the original.

The original American commission was the result of long dissatisfaction with the version of *Cyrano de Bergerac* that Brian Hooker made for Walter Hampden and published in 1923, and which – with many directorial cuts – Michael Langham had used for a production at Stratford, Ontario, in 1963, when Christopher Plummer played the lead for the first time.

The Hooker translation (often termed facetiously the unhappy Hooker) is still the standard version used in America, though my own is beginning to supersede it, and it was the basis for the film of the play in which José Ferrer starred. It achieved a kind of literary sanctity as the Random House Modern Library of the World's Best Books definitive and undislodgeable Everybody's Cyrano, and this status is not undeserved. Hooker was a respectable minor poet, and, like many minor poets of the twenties, very skilful with traditional minor poetic forms like the ballade and the triolet – both represented in *Cyrano* – as well as possessing a knack with blank verse. Moreover, he had the humility to stick very close to Rostand, and he does not cut one line: his translation can very nearly be used as a key to the original. But he was not so slavish as not to recognize that certain literary references in Rostand would not easily be caught by non-French audiences. Thus, in Cyrano's long speech about his nose, he substitutes 'Was this the nose that launched a thousand ships?' for

> Enfin, parodiant Pyrame en un sanglot:
> 'Le voilà donc ce nez qui des traits de son maître
> A détruit l'harmonie! Il en rougit, le traître!'

Here Rostand is referring to a tragedy known to a Paris audience but not to any likely to fill a theatre in London, New York or Minneapolis. Encouraged by Hooker's ingenuity, but unhappy about his failure to render the poignant tone of the original, I tried the following equivalent of the Pyrame parody:

> And finally, with tragic cries and sighs,
> The language finely wrought and deeply felt:
> 'Oh that this too too solid nose would melt!'

But, if I had not read Hooker, I might have translated Rostand's lines more or less literally, thus losing a climax and a comic-heroic effect.

Hooker's translation, then, is both faithful and bold, but it never works on the stage, or on the late-late television screen, with the zing and bite or (since we have to use the word sooner or later when discussing Cyrano or *Cyrano*) panache we have a right to expect. Hooker has produced a play in *cinq actes* and *vers*, but he has not produced a *comédie héroïque*. Rostand is funny, as well as pathetic and sentimental, but Hooker rarely raises a laugh. For that matter, his pathos is sometimes too mawkish for comfort, and when we are moved it is very frequently in spite of the words. The trouble lies, I think, in Hooker's decision to use blank verse, a medium that ceased to be dramatically viable about 1630. Overwhelmingly rich in Shakespeare, solid, chunky, sometimes magnificent in Ben Jonson, packed and astringent in Massinger, blank verse became, in the nineteenth-century revivalist tradition that Hooker followed, an over-limpid or limping medium full of self-conscious Shakespearian echoes and somewhat remote – which the blank verse of the Elizabethans and, even more so, Jacobeans was not – from the rhythms of ordinary speech. Hooker makes Cyrano sound like a man speaking blank verse:

> What would you have me do?
> Seek for the patronage of some great man,
> And like a creeping vine on a tall tree
> Crawl upward, where I cannot stand alone?
> No, thank you! Dedicate, as others do,
> Poems to pawnbrokers? Be a buffoon
> In the vile hope of teasing out a smile
> On some cold face?

Elizabethan characters, on the other hand, sound like men imposing their own idiolects on a fundamental beat of iambic pentameters that is, so to speak, the unconscious and disregarded pulse of the play.

Rostand, of course, wrote in rhymed alexandrines, like the great classical French dramatists, tragic and comic alike, and this metric ought strictly to be rendered into English heroic couplets:

> What would you have me do?
> Seek out a powerful protector, pursue
> A potent patron? Cling like a leeching vine
> To a tree? *Crawl* my way up? Fawn, whine
> For all that sticky candy called success?

> No, thank you. Be a sycophant and dress
> In sickly rhymes a prayer to a moneylender?
> Play the buffoon, desperate to engender
> A smirk on a refrigerated jowl?

Not, certainly, the very regular couplets of Pope, which no living writer can easily imitate, but five-beat lines with a varying number of syllables and a regular couplet rhyming scheme. Sprung or counterpoint rhythm, to use Gerard Manley Hopkins's terms, not strict decasyllables. I read and saw performed Richard Wilbur's translation of Molière's *Tartuffe*, in which he clings doggedly to rhymed decasyllabic couplets, and, in my first draft of *Cyrano* in translation, I tried to follow his example. Christopher Fry's version for the Chichester Theatre is in strict couplets, and I do not think it works any more than my first effort did. French alexandrines can be used in many ways, and the classical comic way, which is Molière's, is conventional, unpoetic, arhetorical: the metric seems to symbolize the social order and it is not available for the special expressive purposes of any individual character. Rostand is a late Romantic, and his alexandrine, though sometimes merely traditional and conventional (the tuning-up violins in Act I have to accommodate their *la* to it), becomes sometimes a highly rhetorical medium as well as a clever instrument of stichomythia. The English heroic couplet, with its mostly intellectual associations, cannot do as much. And the double clop of rhyme, always expected, always fulfilled, though admirable for moral or philosophical discourse, is difficult to sustain in a play which contains a lot of action and sudden surprises.

My final decision was to use *some* rhyme, but to avoid couplets except for Cyrano's big scenes, which have an insolence or lyrical self-confidence to which the relentless unvarying clang of couplets seemed appropriate. Very frequently, the auditor will register rhyme irregularly placed, and for that matter verse rhythm itself, only subliminally. Rhyme is deliberately muffled at times, but there are occasions when it has to assert itself and snap out wittily. Take, for example, the passage in which de Guiche tells Cyrano that, Quixote-like, he is fighting windmills and that it may happen that

> Un moulinet de leurs grands bras chargé de toiles
> Vous lance dans la boue!

To which Cyrano replies: 'Ou bien dans les étoiles!' That is not, by English standards, a true rhyme, but to French ears it is witty, exact and subtly punning. In Hooker's version, de Guiche says that the windmills

> May swing round their huge arms and cast you down
> Into the mire.

And Cyrano answers: 'Or up – among the stars!' This is romantic enough, the tone of a diluted Mercurio, but Cyrano is being neat as well as bold. He needs the wit of rhyme. My version goes:

DE GUICHE. If you fight with windmills, they'll swing their heavy spars
> And spin you down to the mud.
CYRANO.   Or up to the stars.

As Hopkins said of his *Eurydice*, the reader, if he reads the kind of verse I have contrived here with his eyes, and not his ears, will get a brutal impression of 'raw nakedness'. The needs of speaking actors have come before the desire for prosodic neatness. Though I sustain a basic five-beat rhythm throughout the greater part of the translation, this is sometimes deliberately allowed to collapse: in the final act the line often breaks down totally, leaving a gasping kind of *vers libre*. The true test of the verse technique, such as it is, rests in stage performance. This is not a poem but a play.

The very last word spoken by Cyrano before he dies is, in the original, and in my translation too, *panache*. This attribute, he says, is the one thing that death and judgement cannot take away from him. We use the word in English, since there is no native synonym for it, but we cannot always be sure that we are using it in a Rostandian sense. Rostand was kind enough to attempt a definition for the French Academy in 1901:

Le panache n'est pas la grandeur, mais quelque chose qui s'ajoute à la grandeur, et qui bouge au-dessus d'elle. C'est quelque chose de voltigeant, d'excessif, et d'un peu frisé . . . c'est le courage dominant à ce point la situation qu'il en trouve le mot. . . . Certes, les héros sans panache sont plus désintéressés que les autres, car le panache, c'est souvent, dans un sacrifice qu'on fait, une consolation d'attitude qu'on se donne. Un peu frivole peut-être, un peu théâtral sans doute, le panache n'est qu'une grâce; mais cette grâce . . . suppose tant de force (l'esprit qui voltige n'est-il pas la plus belle victoire sur la carcasse qui tremble?) que, tout de même, c'est une grâce que je nous souhaite.

So subtly Gallic a concept cannot easily be conveyed by any English word, except perhaps by something as symbolic as *plume*, or *white plume*, which is what Cyrano flaunts on his hat and, of course, is his literal *panache*. Allowing Cyrano to make his last English word the same as his last French one, I have tried to prepare the audience for its totality of meaning by using it in various contexts (odd lines additional to Rostand's) throughout the play.

Cyrano de Bergerac may not be the greatest play ever written, and this English version is certainly highly supersessible, but I do not think that, when noticing the Royal Shakespeare Company's production, the critic of *The Times Literary Supplement* was in order in suggesting that a highly talented troupe of actors had something better to do with its, and its audience's, time than to put on such rubbish. No play is rubbish if it pleases and if it takes money at the door. The conditions for good dramaturgy are not quite the same as for good fiction or lyric poetry. Dare we despise *The Mouse Trap* for packing them in for thirty-odd years? My first version of *Cyrano* put the Guthrie Theater into the black after years of being in the red. It fulfilled the first rule of the professional drama – to feed the actors. I recognize very clearly the aesthetic faults of *Cyrano de Bergerac* – the bald contrivances, the psychological implausibilities, the gross sentimentality of the ending – but I consider that the leading role is one of the great ones and that Cyrano has something not altogether superficial to say to an age trying to make a style out of despair. The play was worth translating, is worth acting and, I trust you will find, worth reading.

Monaco, April 1984

We are preparing to shoot a film called *Cyrano de Bergerac*: freely adapted from Rostand's play. I don't care to talk much about the play here because, during the past two years of work, throughout the five successive drafts of the script, the play gradually faded in the distance as the vision of a film grew stronger and more tangible. Today, I can no longer tell what is by Rostand, what is by Carrière, and what is by Rappeneau. However, in working out the shot list with my sister Elisabeth these past few weeks, I was overwhelmed by the constant feeling of setting a marvellous story to images. But this film, because you mustn't forget we are dealing with a film, will have a particularity: the characters speak in verse. For a long time this has frightened a number of people. Several producers who were tempted by the project ended up shelving it for they felt the challenge impossible to meet. But all films today are alike. We are flooded with sounds and images that are all the same. As soon as you see two shots of a film, you hear two lines of dialogue, you know what comes next. Then all you can do is change the channel or walk out of the theatre. Today, as you know, only films that have something different can captivate the audience. *Cyrano de Bergerac* won't be like any other film. We think that its rhyming dialogue, its sudden flourishes, these alexandrines cut in two, three, four and sometimes even five phrases, this vertiginously acrobatic ping-pong will be the key to the film's success. So what will we do with this verse? How will we deal with these wayward alexandrines, so different from those of Racine and Corneille, but that descend rather from Victor Hugo's Romantic drama? I'm not an acting teacher, I have no theories, I have no guidelines, and furthermore there aren't any reliable ones that work in all circumstances. The only thing I possess is an ear, and I trust it. Some actors and actresses whom I won't name and who I obviously didn't hire told me, after reading the script: 'No problem, it's just like prose.' But no, precisely, it isn't at all like prose, and if we make the verse sound too commonplace, we will diminish it and all the charm will vanish. French poetry is based on count, and here the count is twelve. But if we go to the other extreme, if we emphasize each line, each break, if we hammer out each of these twelve syllables, the film won't hold up. It will fall apart, shattered by its own metrics. Finally, what I want is for the verse to be present in an absent manner, like music in the background heard throughout a film, sometimes faintly, amplified at others. That's right, I'm searching for a music, a sound, a harmony.

Jean-Paul Rappeneau

Cyrano de Bergerac : The Film

Cast

CYRANO DE BERGERAC	Gerard Depardieu
ROXANE	Anne Brochet
CHRISTIAN DE NEUVILLETTE	Vincent Perez
COMTE DE GUICHE	Jacques Weber
RAGUENEAU	Roland Bertin
LE BRET	Philippe Morier-Genoud
CARBON DE CASTEL-JALOUX	Pierre Maguelon
THE DUENNA	Josiane Stoleru
THE CHILD	Anatole Delalande
THE LITTLE SISTER	Ludivine Sagnier
THE FATHER	Alain Rimoux
VICOMTE DE VALVERT	Philippe Volter
LIGNIERE	Jean-Marie Winling
THE BORE	Louis Navarre
MONTFLEURY	Gabriel Monnet
BELLEROSE	Francois Marie
JODELET	Pierre Triboulet
FIRST SOLDIER	Baptiste Roussillon
SECOND SOLDIER	Christian Roy
THE FOOTPAD	Jacques Pater
FIRST MARQUIS	Pierre Aussedat
SECOND MARQUIS	Yves Aubert
THE ACADEMICIAN	Lucien Pascal
CONCEITED YOUNG MAN	Jean-Damien Barbin
THE MONK	Jerome Nicolin
THE MATRON	Nicole Felix
THE CADETS	Christian Loustau, Alain Perez
	Franck Jazede, Eric Bernard
	Franck Ramon, Alain Dumas
	Herve Pauchon
DE GUICHE'S OFFICER	Philippe Girard
BAKER'S BOY	Quentin Ogier
LISE RAGUENEAU	Catherine Ferran
RAGUENEAU'S 1ST POET	Vincent Nemeth
RAGUENEAU'S 2ND POET	Michel Fau
URANIE	Christine Culerier
GREMIONE	Cecile Camp
LYSIMON	Benoit Vergne
FIRST 'PRECIOUS' POET	Eric Picou
SECOND 'PRECIOUS' POET	Eric Frey
MOTHER SUPERIOR	Madeleine Marion
SISTER MARTHE	Amelie Gonin
SISTER COLETTE	Sandrine Kiberlain
SISTER CLAIRE	Isabelle Gruault
IRONING NUN	Louise Vincent
BAD-TEMPERED NUN	Claudine Gabay

Produced by	Rene Cleitman and Michel Seydoux
Directed by	Jean-Paul Rappeneau
Based on the play by	Edmond Rostand
Screenplay and adaptation	Jean-Paul Rappeneau
	Jean-Claude Carriere
Music composed and directed by	Jean-Claude Petit
Director of photography	Pierre Lhomme
Cameramen	Yves Agostini and Janos Kende
Production designer	Ezio Frigerio
Costumes by	Franca Squarciapino
Sound engineer	Pierre Gamet
Fencing master	William Hobbs
Design for Cyrano's nose	Michele Burke
Hairstyle and wig design	Paul Leblanc
Make-up artist	Jean-Pierre Eychenne
Hairdresser	Pierre Vade
Editor	Noelle Boisson
Sound editor	Jean Goudier
English Subtitles	Anthony Burgess

A Hachette Premiere & Cie/Camera One/Films A2/
DD Productions/U.G.C. Co-productions
An Artificial Eye Release

Cyrano de Bergerac required 2000 actors and extras, 2000 costumes, half of which were specially designed for the film; a genuine arsenal, including 300 swords, 500 pikes, 150 muskets, 100 pistols, 2 howitzers, and a dozen canons, over 1000 weapons in all; 40 studio sets and outdoor locations, as well as planting of several acres to recreate the vegetation for the siege of Arras; widening a river, and redesigning an entire forest. All in all, it involved means heretofore unmatched in the history of French cinema.

The movie, 2 hours and 15 minutes long, was shot partly in Hungary (Budapest, the vicinity of Budapest, the Eger region) and in France (Le Mans, Fontainebleau, Moret-sur-Loing, Fontenay, Dijon, Uzès).

THE CHARACTERS

Named	Unnamed
Cyrano de Bergerac	Doorkeeper
Christian de Neuvillette	a Cavalryman
Comte de Guiche	a Musketeer
Ragueneau	Another Musketeer (believed
Le Bret	to be d'Artagnan)
Carbon de Castel-Jaloux	a Guard
Vicomte de Valvert	a Fat Man
Montfleury	a Citizen
Bellerose	His Son
Jodelet	a Drunkard
Cuigy	a Pickpocket
Lignière	His Apprentices
Brissaille	Two Flunkeys
Théophraste Renaudot	Two Boys (pages at the
Bertrandou the Fluteplayer	theatre, customers at
	Ragueneau's shop,
	eventually musicians)
	Other Pages
	Two Marquises
	a Capuchin
	a Sentry
	the Poets
	a Poet
	Pastrycooks
	Cadets
	a Spanish Officer
Roxane	Roxane's Duenna (eventually
Lise	Sister Marthe)
Mother Marquérite de Jésus	Flowergirl
Sister Marthe	Foodseller
Sister Claire	Actresses

*The Crowd, Marquises, Thieves, Actors,
Musicians, Précieuses, Nuns, etc.*

Anthony Burgess's translation of Rostand's *Cyrano de Bergerac* was commissioned by the Royal Shakespeare Company and first staged at the Barbican Theatre, London on 21 July 1983. The cast, in order of appearance, was as follows:

THE DOORKEEPER	Jimmy Gardner
A CAVALRYMAN	Richard Clifford
D'ARTAGNAN	Robert Clare
TWO FLUNKEYS	Philip Dennis, Brian Parr
A MUSKETEER	Geoffrey Freshwater
A FLOWER GIRL	Lesley Sharp
AN EATER	Niall Padden
A DRINKER	Phillip Walsh
A CITIZEN	Simon Clark
HIS SON	Paul Russell
TWO PAGES	William Adams, Rupert Baderman John Holmes, Claire Smith
A PICKPOCKET	Ray Llewellyn
TWO MARQUISES	Jeffery Dench, David Glover
CUIGY	Dennis Clinton
BRISAILLE	Raymond Bowers
LIGNIERE THE POET	George Parsons
BARON CHRISTIAN DE NEUVILLETTE, a Norman	Floyd Bevan
A FOOD SELLER	Cathy Finlay
RAGUENEAU, a pastry cook	Pete Postlethwaite
LE BRET	John Bowe
ROXANE, Cyrano's cousin	Alice Krige
HER DUENNA	Jennie Goossens
LE COMTE DE GUICHE	John Carlisle
LE VICOMTE DE VALVERT	Christopher Bowen
MONTFLEURY, a tragic actor	Michael Fitzgerald
CYRANO DE BERGERAC, a Gascon	Derek Jacobi
BELLEROSE, leader of the acting company	David Shaw-Parker
JODELET, the comedian	Tom Mannion
PRÉCIEUSES	Penelope Beaumont, Alexandra Brook, Clare Byam Shaw
LISE, Ragueneau's Wife	Penelope Beaumont
CARBON DE CASTEL JALOUX, Captain of the Gascony Cadets	Ken Bones
THE GASCONY CADETS	Niall Padden, Tom Mannion, Christopher Bowen, Richard Clifford, Brian Parr, David Shaw-Parker, Robert Clare, Philip Dennis
THÉOPHRASTE RENAUDOT, a journalist	Phillip Walsh
A CAPUCHIN	Jimmy Gardner
MOTHER MARGUÉRITE	Penelope Beaumont
SISTER MARTHE	Cathy Finlay
SISTER CLAIRE	Lesley Sharp

Actors, Nuns, Pastry Cooks, Poets, Soldiers,
played by members of the Company

Directed by Terry Hands
Designed by Ralph Koltai
Costumes by Alexander Reid
Music by Nigel Hess

Lighting by Terry Hands *with* Clive Morris
Fights arranged by Ian McKay
Cyrano's nose by Christopher Tucker

Act I

A theatre

We are in Paris in 1640, the era of Dumas's Three
Musketeers. *The theatre is not a theatre as we know theatres. It
is rather like a large indoor tennis court roughly converted into a
place where plays may be performed before small audiences, or
chamber concerts given for even fewer. There is a platform which
serves as a stage, and a number of benches accommodate the less
patrician spectators. The gentry and aristocracy will be seated in a
low gallery with chairs, while a higher one, chairless, from which
the view is not good, is intended for their servants. It is evening.
The lights have not yet been lit, and a huge candelabrum has still
to be raised by its heavy rope to the ceiling. The shadows invite
lovers and lechers. Such illumination as there is is provided by
odd candles and lanterns set about the floor and on chairs. A*
PICKPOCKET *instructs his pupils in the art they must practise this
evening. A* DOORKEEPER *takes tickets or, from the ticketless,
money. A* CAVALRYMAN *pushes his way in past him.*

DOORKEEPER. Hey – where's your fifteen sous?
CAVALRYMAN.   I get in free.
DOORKEEPER. And why?
CAVALRYMAN.   His Majesty's Household Cavalry.

    Another man in uniform enters boldly. He is a MUSKETEER.

DOORKEEPER. You –

MUSKETEER.   I don't pay either.

DOORKEEPER.   Now look here –

MUSKETEER. *You* look, friend. See – I'm a musketeer.

CAVALRYMAN (*to the* MUSKETEER).

  Ten minutes before curtain-up. The floor
  Is ours.

MUSKETEER. So – what are we waiting for?

> *They draw their épées and start to fence. A* FLUNKEY *comes out of the shadows to watch them. Another* FLUNKEY *appears and addresses the first.*

SECOND FLUNKEY. Pssst – see what I've got –

> *It is not easy to see what he has in the dimness.*

FIRST FLUNKEY. Champagne?

SECOND FLUNKEY.   Cards. Dice.
  What'll it be?

FIRST FLUNKEY (*taking the cards*).

                        I'll deal.

SECOND FLUNKEY.   I nicked a slice
  Of candle. See.

> *He lights it from a candle already lighted and sticks it on a bench.*

                See.

> *Now they can see well enough to play. A town* GUARD *appears from the shadows and makes for a* FLOWERGIRL *who has just come in with her basket of spring blooms.*

GUARD. Come on – here's a nice
  Little bit of dark, dear. Give us a kiss.

CAVALRYMAN (*lunging*).   Touché!

GUARD (*embracing her*).

  Come on.

FLOWERGIRL. They can see.
FIRST FLUNKEY.   One club.
GUARD.   No danger.

A FAT MAN, seated, takes out a cold fowl and a loaf.

FAT MAN.   May
As well get a snack in.

A CITIZEN, decently but drably dressed, enters with his
SON, a lad of about seventeen, drably but decently dressed.
The CITIZEN peers in the dim light.

CITIZEN.   Come on, son – this way.
DRUNKARD (*to the eater*).
What's this place called, then?
FAT MAN.   Theatre Beaujolais.

The DRUNKARD produces a bottle.

DRUNKARD. A good idea.
SECOND FLUNKEY.   Three aces.
CITIZEN (*indignantly*).   You'd think that this
Was a brothel –
GUARD.   Come on, give us a kiss.
CITIZEN. God in heaven – playing cards where they play
Corneille.
HIS SON. Racine as well.

The GUARD gets his kiss, a long one, and the CITIZEN sees
it.

CITIZEN.   Son, look the other way.
SON. Racine's a bit of a bore, though, to be truthful.

Some PAGES enter, singing a rude song. The DOORKEEPER
looks on them with disapproval.

DOORKEEPER. All right, you pages, cut that out.

FIRST PAGE. Just youthful
exuberance, monsieur.
SECOND PAGE. String?
FIRST PAGE (*showing a length of it and also* ...).
And a hook.
DOORKEEPER (*muttering*). Young pigs.
SECOND PAGE. Let's get up there and start to fish for wigs.

They boisterously make their way to the upper gallery. The
PICKPOCKET *addresses his* APPRENTICES *weightily.*

PICKPOCKET. Now, you young villains, novices in crime,
You're performing in public for the very first time –
SECOND PAGE. Peashooters at the ready –
THIRD PAGE. Launch your peas.

The first and second PAGES *hit pates with their peashooters.*
The DOORKEEPER *shakes a furious fist at them.*

CITIZEN'S SON. I've forgotten what they're doing tonight.
CITIZEN. *Clorise.*
PICKPOCKET.
Don't cut the lace too close. The important factor's
Lightness of touch.
CITIZEN. With some really exquisite actors –
PICKPOCKET. Now, as for nicking watches –
CITIZEN. Yes, you'll see
Montfleury –
PICKPOCKET. Tonight, watch me –
CITIZEN. Bellerose, L'Épy –
VOICE. Lights! Lights!
CITIZEN. Le Beaupré, Jodelet –
FIRST PAGE. There she is!

He means a very pretty girl who has appeared from the
shadows with a trolley on which food and drink are set.

FOODSELLER. Cider, raspberry cordial, oranges!

FIRST MARQUIS (*off*).
  Make way, there!

> *He enters with another* MARQUIS. *After these enter* CUIGY *and* BRISSAILLE, *mere gentlemen, and, a little after,* LIGNIÈRE, *a poet who has the face of a distinguished drunkard. He accompanies* CHRISTIAN DE NEUVILLETTE, *a young baron from the north, very handsome, soldierly, his civilian dress somewhat out of the fashion.*

FIRST FLUNKEY. What's this? – marquises? – in the pit?
SECOND MARQUIS. Make room, will you? Animals!
SECOND FLUNKEY.   Oh, just for a bit.
  Then they get sort of elevated.
FIRST MARQUIS.   Scum.
  It's positively obscene, really, to come
  In early like this with the shopkeepers. Why,
  There aren't even any decent feet to tread on. Ah, Brissaille,
  Cuigy –

> *Affectionate greetings.*

CUIGY.   My dear. We're here with the
    devout,
  Before even the candles are lit.
FIRST MARQUIS.   Pooh!
SECOND MARQUIS.   Come, don't pout.
  The lights are coming on now.

> *So they are. The candelabrum is illuminated with care and raised during what follows.* LIGNIÈRE *is now clearly visible.*

CUIGY.   Ah, Lignière!
LIGNIÈRE (*to* CHRISTIAN).
  An introduction?

> CHRISTIAN *shrugs, then nods.*

BRISSAILLE (*to* LIGNIÈRE).
                Not under the table yet?

LIGNIÈRE ignores the remark and formally introduces CHRISTIAN.

LIGNIÈRE. May I present the Baron de Neuvillette?

The crowd expresses its delight by going 'Aaaah!' as the lights grow brighter and brighter. The MARQUISES and CUIGY appraise CHRISTIAN.

CUIGY. A charming head of hair on the boy, yes?
FIRST MARQUIS (*doubtfully*).   Well –
LIGNIÈRE.   Messieurs
De Cuigy, de Brissaille –
CHRISTIAN.   Enchanté.
FIRST MARQUIS.   Pretty
Enough, but rather provincial.
SECOND MARQUIS.   Hm, a pity.

LIGNIÈRE hears the remark about CHRISTIAN's provinciality.

LIGNIÈRE. The baron comes from Touraine.
CUIGY.   Really?
CHRISTIAN.   Well,
yes.
CUIGY. A stranger to Paris?
CHRISTIAN.   I've been here rather less
Than three weeks.

These aristocrats fluster him, and he has something else on his mind.

I'm joining the Guards.

The ladies of wit and fashion have arrived and are taking their places in the lower gallery.

FIRST MARQUIS.   There she is –
Madame Aubry.

FOODSELLER.   Lemonade, oranges.

STRINGS (*tuning up*).
La. La. Laaaaaa –

CUIGY (*to* CHRISTIAN).
                    Quite a crowd here, eh?

CHRISTIAN. Indeed.

FIRST MARQUIS.   The *bon ton.*

SECOND MARQUIS.   Madame de Guéméné –

CUIGY. De Bois-Dauphin –

FIRST MARQUIS.   Whom once we were crazy for –

BRISSAILLE. De Chauvigny –

SECOND MARQUIS.   Who treats our hearts like the
     floor.

LIGNIÈRE. Corneille has come from Rouen.

CITIZEN.   The Academy?
There they are, most of them. Can you see?
Boudu, Boissat, Cureau, Forchères, Colomby,
Bourzeys, Bourdon, Arbaud – what an honour to sit
Near names that can never die. Just think of it.

We cannot see these personages, since they are all some-
where in our auditorium. We are not missing much,
however. But we do see the very special ladies of wit and
fashion now enter.

FIRST MARQUIS. Ah, here they come – our *précieuses* –

CHRISTIAN (*to* LIGNIÈRE).   What
     are those?

LIGNIÈRE. Beautiful bluestockings.

CHRISTIAN (*mystified*)   What?

FIRST MARQUIS.   Ah – there she
     goes.
Barthénoïde, and there's Félixérie –
Urimédonte, Cassadance –

LIGNIÈRE.   To me
They sound like high-class diseases.

SECOND MARQUIS (*to* FIRST MARQUIS).

                             Exquisite

  Pseudonyms. You know them all?

FIRST MARQUIS.   I admit

  To trying to know them all.

LIGNIÈRE (*somewhat irritably, to* CHRISTIAN).

                       Look, I came here

  To help you if I could. But it's pretty clear

  That the lady isn't coming. I'll be on my way –

  I've some serious drinking to do tonight.

CHRISTIAN (*urgently*).   No, stay

  Just a while longer. *Please*. To nurse a flame

  Like mine for a . . .

He has difficulty, as always, in finding the right word.

LIGNIÈRE.   Woman without a name?

The ORCHESTRA LEADER *has come in, to no applause. He chins his fiddle, raises his bow.*

ORCHESTRA LEADER. Gentlemen of the orchestra –

He gives the downbeat, and they play soft preludial music.

FOODSELLER.   Lemonade.

  Macaroons.

CHRISTIAN.   You'll know her. I'm afraid,

  Afraid she'll be coquettish, exquisite –

  Afraid to speak and show my . . .

LIGNIÈRE.   Lack of wit.

CHRISTIAN. This smart new language they all speak and

    write

  Eludes me. All I know is . . .

LIGNIÈRE (*promptly*).   How to fight.

A soldier conquered by two enemies –
Shyness and love.

CHRISTIAN.   I *must* know who she is.
Wait till she comes – she's bound to come –

LIGNIÈRE.   Oh, no.
Thirst waits for no man. Sorry, I must go –
I've the whole of Paris to swim through.

> The FOODSELLER *brightly accosts him.*

FOODSELLER.   Orangeade?

LIGNIÈRE (*shuddering*). Oh God.

FOODSELLER   Milk?
                              My sweet young
    dairymaid,

LIGNIÈRE.
I was weaned a long long time back.

FOODSELLER.   Muscadel?

LIGNIÈRE. Hm. Sweetish, sweetish. Very well,
Christian, I'll stay awhile.

> He sits on the edge of a bench and the FOODSELLER *pours*
> *him a large glass. Meanwhile* RAGUENEAU *has entered –*
> *portly, dressed in a Sunday suit, well pleased with himself,*
> *acknowledging the recognition of the crowd.*

LIGNIÈRE.   Ah, Ragueneau.
(*To* CHRISTIAN)
This is the man who lets you eat and owe,
If you're a poet.

RAGUENEAU.   Monsieur Lignière,
Have you seen Monsieur de Bergerac anywhere?

LIGNIÈRE. The prince of pastrycooks.

RAGUENEAU.   Oh, really, now –

LIGNIÈRE. Quiet, you patron of the tarts, arts.

RAGUENEAU.   I allow
That poets honour my establishment.

LIGNIÈRE   On credit.
  He's a talented poet himself.
RAGUENEAU.   Well, some have said it.
LIGNIÈRE. Cracked, aren't you, crazy about the art?
RAGUENEAU. Well –
LIGNIÈRE.   For an ode he'll pay a rhubarb tart.
RAGUENEAU. Let's say a tartlet.
LIGNIÈRE.   And a sonnet?
RAGUENEAU.   A small
  Swiss roll.
LIGNIÈRE. As for a play –
RAGUENEAU.   The drama – ah, my soul
  Seethes.
LIGNIÈRE. Damp your oven, sir. Gâteaux and such
  Buy him his theatre tickets. Tell us how much
  It cost you to come tonight.
RAGUENEAU.   Four fruit flans,
  Six cream buns. Where's Cyrano?
LIGNIÈRE.   That man's
  Not much of a theatregoer.

  He is now on his third glass.

RAGUENEAU.   Oh, but he's
  Got to be here.
LIGNIÈRE.   *Got* to be?
RAGUENEAU.   Montfleury's
  Performing.
LIGNIÈRE.   True, treading a tragic measure,
  Three hundred pounds of pork *en gelée*. So?
RAGUENEAU. Cyrano has warned him – surely you know? –
  To quit the stage on pain of his displeasure
  For a whole month.
BRISSAILLE.   And, to quote Lignière, so?
RAGUENEAU. Montfleury's performing.
CUIGY.   An empty sort of
    veto,
  Surely.

RAGUENEAU.   I think not, gentlemen, oh no.
That's why I'm here. Where is he?
FIRST MARQUIS.   This Cyrano –
What is he?
CUIGY.   A sort of metal merchant.
SECOND MARQUIS.   Oh,
Not aristocratic, then?
CUIGY.   Sufficiently so.
He's in the Guards. But there's his friend Le Bret.

*He refers to a good solid captain of the Guards, who is
pacing up and down nervously.*

Le Bret, come over. What have you to say
About this Cyrano business?

LE BRET comes over to the group.

LE BRET.   Oh God.
CUIGY.   I see.
LE BRET. I'm worried.
BRISSAILLE.   You have every right to be.

But RAGUENEAU has been smiling.

RAGUENEAU. What an extraordinary man he is.
LE BRET. Exquisite – one of the world's prodigies.
RAGUENEAU. Poet.
CUIGY.   Fighter.
BRISSAILLE.   Physician.
LE BRET.   Musician.
LIGNIÈRE.   Ah –
His appearance, though – isn't that truly bizarre?
RAGUENEAU. Bizarre, excessive, hyperbolic, droll,
With his triple-waving plume, his visible soul,
Six slashes in his doublet, and his cloak,
Which the flashing scabbard hoists up at the back
To make it like the tail of a barnyard cock –

That is Cyrano de Bergerac.
Cocky, insolent, Gascony-proud he goes,
Flaunting that Punchinello strawberry nose
Of his – a nose, gentlemen, that makes one feel
Like squealing: 'Oh God, no, it can't be real.
It must be detachable – *is*, I'm prepared to bet.'
But Cyrano's never been known to detach it yet.

LE BRET. He wears it, or it him, and, should anyone laugh,
His sword swoops down and lops him clean in half.

RAGUENEAU. That blade is one of the blades of destiny's
scissors.

FIRST MARQUIS. But he doesn't seem to be coming.

LE BRET.   Oh, yes
he is, as
Sure as my name's –

RAGUENEAU.   He'll be here in a minute
or so. I'm prepared to bet a *poulet Ragueneau*.

To universal admiration Roxane enters with her DUENNA.
CHRISTIAN, *who is paying for* LIGNIÈRE'*s wine, does not see
her. But everybody else does.*

SECOND MARQUIS. Look at her – how unbearably beautiful –
FIRST MARQUIS. A strawberry mouth in peach-flesh.
SECOND MARQUIS.   So
fresh, so cool,
She'd give one cardiac rheumatism.

CHRISTIAN *sees her, is speechless, clutches* LIGNIÈRE *and
points tremulously.*

LIGNIÈRE.   Ah. so
That's the one.

CHRISTIAN.   Yes yes yes, who? Tell me – oh,
My knees are knocking.

LIGNIÈRE.   Second name – Robin.
Known as Roxane, though christened Madeleine.

CHRISTIAN (*ardently*).
Roxane!

LIGNIÈRE.   Roxana really. You know –
Alexander's mistress.

> CHRISTIAN, *in a transport of jealousy, prepares to draw his sword.*

CHRISTIAN.   Alexander!
LIGNIÈRE.   Wait.
He's dead. He's safe. He used to be called the Great.
Delicately reared. Bookish.
CHRISTIAN.   Bookish? Oh no.
LIGNIÈRE. Still single. An orphan. Cousin to the Cyrano
We were talking about just now.

> *A nobleman is to be seen paying her every courtly attention.*

CHRISTIAN.   Who's that with her?

> LIGNIÈRE *takes a deep draught and then launches into alexandrines.*

LIGNIÈRE. That's the Comte de Guiche, complete with
cordon bleu,
Totally smitten with her but irreparably wed
To the niece of none other than Cardinal Richelieu.
If he can't marry Roxane, he proposes to hitch her
instead
To a certain unpleasant viscount – there he is – Valvert.
The viscount is – complaisant. So de Guiche will push in
there
If you catch my meaning. She comes of the bourgeoisie,
And de Guiche could unleash, if he wished, such
concentrated hell
As to make her wish she'd never been born. Ah well,
That's de Guiche, the swine. He has it in for me.
I wrote a little song about him showing
Up his piggish machiavellianisms. I'll sing it.
CHRISTIAN.   No, I'm
going
To to to –

But LIGNIÈRE *with drunkard's strength holds on to him.*

LIGNIÈRE.　　　　　You're going to listen. Listen.

He sings in a cracked voice.

> The bite of that
> Aristocrat,
> Like any other sewer rat,
> Infects the gut
> With such a glut
> Of venom in the groin or gut
> That, so they tell,
> The victims yell
> Not from the pain but from the smell.

CHRISTIAN *tears himself away.*

CHRISTIAN. Let's get it over now, once and for ever –
LIGNIÈRE.　　　　　　　　　　　　　　Who?
CHRISTIAN. This Viscount de Valvert.
LIGNIÈRE.　　　　　　　　　　Idiot. Small stuff
　　like you –
　　He'll eat you in canapés. Stop it. And see –
　　She's looking at you.
CHRISTIAN (*enraptured*).　Oh heavens, it's true.
　At me. At me. God, she's looking at me.
LIGNIÈRE. So – me and my thirst – we'll be the ones to go.

He zigzags off. The chief PICKPOCKET *takes advantage of* CHRISTIAN's *ecstasy to sidle towards him. The* APPRENTICE PICKPOCKETS *look at their master's behest. A lesson.*

LE BRET. No Cyrano.
RAGUENEAU.　　　　　I can't understand it.
LE BRET.　　　　　　　　　　　Oh,
　　It's possible he hasn't seen the playbill.

The SPECTATORS *are growing impatient. They yell.*

SPECTATORS. Begin! Begin! Begin!

LE BRET.   I hope that's so.

FIRST MARQUIS. Keeps quite a court, de Guiche.

> DE GUICHE *is indeed the centre of a number of sycophants.*
> *He stands chatting with them at the pit level in front of the*
> *lower gallery.*

SECOND MARQUIS.   Another
  one

Of these Gascons – supple, cold, able.

No doubt about it, marquis, they get on.

Shall we pay our respects?

> *The other nods and they trip over to* DE GUICHE *to admire*
> *his exquisite clothes.*

FIRST MARQUIS.   Such lovely ribbons, sir.

What is this colour called? Kiss–me–my–dear?

Or startled–fawn?

DE GUICHE.   Sick Spaniard.

SECOND MARQUIS.   Ah, that colour

Tells no lie. Thanks to your lordship's valour,

The Spanish force in Flanders, so we hear,

Will soon be very sick.

DE GUICHE.   I must take my place

Up there. Coming?

> *He goes towards the stage where, in the Elizabethan*
> *manner, chairs are set for a few of the better sort. He sees*
> VALVERT *hanging back, eyes on* ROXANE.

                 Coming? *Coming, Valvert?*

> VALVERT *shakes himself out of his absorption and follows*
> *his patron. Hearing the name,* CHRISTIAN *trembles with*
> *rage.*

CHRISTIAN. Good as dead. Let me hurl it in his face,

  My –

He puts his hand in his pocket but finds the PICKPOCKET's *already there. The neophytes are shocked by their master's ineptitude.*

PICKPOCKET (*amiably*).
   Quite a crush tonight. We're practically
   In one another's pockets.
CHRISTIAN.   So I see.
   I was looking for a glove.
PICKPOCKET.   And you've found a mitt.

His sick and piteous smirk changes. He speaks urgently.

   I didn't have no intention – It was just a bit
   Of (ow!) fun –

   CHRISTIAN *holds on to the mitt, hard.*

                    Let me go, sir, and I'll let
   (Ow!) you into a secret –
CHRISTIAN.   Secret? What? *What?*

He hangs on to the hand but lets it gradually go during the following.

PICKPOCKET.   That Lignière – him who's just left – he's not
   Got more than an hour to live. He wrote a song
   Attacking one of these gents, who's sending along
   A hundred men to get him. I'm one. That's how
   I know, you see.
CHRISTIAN.   What 'gent'?
PICKPOCKET.   Oh really, now –
   Professional discretion –
CHRISTIAN.   Where will they be?
PICKPOCKET.   The Porte de Nesle. That's on his way home,
      see.
   You'd better get a message to him.
CHRISTIAN.   How
   Am I going to find him?

PICKPOCKET. Start off now.
Try all the public houses – the Red Cow,
The Broken Corset, Pineapple – try the lot,
Jot down a message. Quick, though. Soon he'll not
Be able to read.

Freed, the PICKPOCKET *shamefacedly returns to his little troupe.* CHRISTIAN *is greatly agitated.*

CHRISTIAN. Cowards! A hundred men
Against one poet. Oh, to have to leave just when
I've found her. Him. Her. She. He.
Lignière comes first. Where the hell will he be?

He dashes off. The theatre is now full and very impatient.

SPECTATORS. Begin! Begin!

A man has his wig fished off.

FIRST PAGE. Look at him – bald as a bat!

There is joyous laughter, which is suddenly hushed to a silence. LE BRET *is puzzled.*

LE BRET. Why?

The CITIZEN *whispers to him.*

Here? Him? You're sure of that?
CITIZEN. Would you like a signed certificate?
DRUNKARD. *Mon Dieu* –
Up in that sort of confession-box – Richelieu.

He makes the sign of the cross. Richelieu is somewhere high on the fourth wall.

FIRST PAGE. The cardinal, damn it. Now there's no more
fun.
FIRST MARQUIS. Pass me that chair there.
A SPECTATOR. Quiet, everyone.

The baton raps three times. Music.

LE BRET. He comes on now?

RAGUENEAU.   He starts it off. Very odd.
  No Cyrano. I've lost my bet.

LE BRET (*fervently but* sotto voce). Thank God.

> MONTFLEURY *waddles on, escorted by nymphs. He is
> grotesquely fat and wears a stylized shepherd's costume with
> rustic bagpipes under his arm. He graciously acknowledges
> the applause.*

SPECTATORS. Montfleury – good old Montfleury!

MONTFLEURY. Far from the court and city, ah – how good
  To breathe the incense of the verdant wood,
  While cool harmonious breezes seem to say –

VOICE. Fat fool, I ordered you to stay away.

> *The* VOICE *utters the line in the same exaggerated stagy
> manner as* MONTFLEURY. *People look everywhere for the
> owner of the voice. He is in the auditorium (ours).*

CUIGY. It's him –

LE BRET.   God help us all –

VOICE.   Balloon, baboon,
  Buffoon, for the space of one revolving moon
  I ordered you to *rest*. You hesitate?
  Get off that stage.

SPECTATORS.   Don't let him intimidate
  You, Montfleury. Play – continue – carry on –

> *But* MONTFLEURY's *confidence is somewhat diminished.*

MONTFLEURY. Far from the court and city, ah – how –

VOICE.   Good!
  You see this stick, you clown? I'll plant a wood,
  Splinter by splinter, over your rich terrain.

MONTFLEURY. Far from the sort and kitty –

VOICE.   Yet again
  You disobey?

  CYRANO, *first made manifest by voice, then by stick,*
  appears personally, nose flaring, and leaps onto a chair.

MONTFLEURY (*tremulously*). Please help me, gentlemen.
FIRST MARQUIS. Carry on acting.
CYRANO.   Not for four more weeks.
  One word more, and I lambast his shivering cheeks,
  All four of them.
SECOND MARQUIS. Enough.

  Some of the aristocracy rise in protest.

CYRANO.   Stay in your stalls,
  You vaccine marquises. Your mooing calls
  My cane to rummage through your folderols.
DE GUICHE. This is too much. Continue, Montfleury.
CYRANO. Discontinue, rather, unless he,
  Unwilling to retire to sty or trough,
  Needs disembowelling and his jowls cut off.
  Off, off, you offal. Lug your guts away,
  You mortadella. Very well, then – stay,
  And I'll remove you slice by slice.

  MONTFLEURY *summons up the remains of his dignity.*

MONTFLEURY.   Monsieur,
  In insulting me you insult the Tragic Muse.

  There are some murmurs of agreement and admiration.

CYRANO (*equably*).
  If the Tragic Muse had the dubious honour, fat sir,
  Of your acquaintance, she would not abuse
  Her pious duty. Seeing the blubber ooze
  Into your collar and your belly round as a clock,
  She'd kick your buttocks with her tragic sock.

CITIZEN (*leading the pit*).
  Carry on, Montfleury – let's hear the play.
CYRANO (*kindly*).
  Consider my poor scabbard, please, I pray.
  She loves my sword and wants my sword to stay
  Inside her. Off that stage! A bleat? A bray?
  Do any of you have anything to say?
VOICE.
                    Where's your authority?
                      You go away.
                    We, the majority,
                      Paid for a play.
THE PIT. That's right – the play, the play – play the play!
CYRANO. If I hear this scrannel song once more there'll be
  A one-man massacre.
CITIZEN.   You're Samson, eh?
CYRANO (*reasonably*).
  Lend me your jawbone, sir, and you'll soon see.
A LADY. Disgraceful.
CITIZEN.   Shocking.
FIRST MARQUIS.   Scandalous.
FIRST PAGE.   Good fun.

  The crowd makes animal noises at CYRANO, *who is
  unperturbed.*

CYRANO. Silence!

  He gets it.

                    I hereby herewith issue one
  Collective challenge. How about you? Or you?
  Come on, now, who'll be first to breathe his last?
  I'll make a list. To every – er – duellist
  I'll award the funeral honours that are his due.
  Raise your right hands, all those who wish to die.
  Is it *pudeur* makes you not wish to eye

My naked blade? Does no one wish to engage
In a metallic romp? Good. Let me say this: I
Want something desperately simple – to see the stage
Rid of this haemorrhoid, goitre, abscess, tumour.
And if the flux won't go of its own free will –
Well, then – the lancet. Buffoon, are you there still?
Please don't presume too much on my good humour.
I'll clap my hands three times, you moon of a man.
Eclipse yourself on the third clap. Ready? One –

MONTFLEURY. I, I –

FIRST MARQUIS.   Don't leave.

PIT.   Go. Don't go.

MONTFLEURY.   It seems to me –

CYRANO. Two.

MONTFLEURY.   On mature consideration –

CYRANO.   Three.

> MONTFLEURY *disappears with, for his bulk, remarkable speed. There is a storm of roars and whistles.*

SPECTATORS. Coward, come back, you coward, coward,
  come back!

CYRANO. Let him if he dares.

CITIZEN.   Monsieur er Bergerac,
  This is irregular. I demand a few words
  From the head of the company.

SPECTATORS.   Bellerose!

> BELLEROSE *comes on and looks doubtfully at everybody.*

BELLEROSE.   My lords,
  Ladies and gentlemen – one hardly knows what to say.

MUSKETEER. Jodelet!

SPECTATORS.   Jodelet! Bring on Jodelet!

> JODELET *slouches on and looks contemptuously at the spectators. But contempt is part of his act and they enjoy it.*

JODELET. You flock of muttonheads –

SPECTATORS.   Bravo! Bravo!

JODELET (*with a strong nasal intonation*).

Let's have no bravos. The distinguished Thespian
Whose paunch you love so much has had to go.

MUSKETEER. He's scared.

JODELET.   Be charitable. Say he's a sick man.

CITIZEN'S SON (*to* CYRANO).

But what are your reasons, sir? Why do you show
Such enmity towards Montfleury?

CYRANO (*courteously*).

                                        Young ninny,
I have two reasons, but let one suffice.
This Montfleury of yours is a deplorable
Mouther, grunter, grimacer, posturer,
Who tears his lines to shivers with a tinny
Voice like a randy cageful of white mice.
The second reason? That's my secret.

CITIZEN.   Intolerable
To deprive us without scruple of a play
As great as *Clorise* –

CYRANO (*respectfully*).

                        The work to which you refer,
You ass, is worth rather less than an ass's bray.
I silenced it without compunction. Sir.

A PRÉCIEUSE. Did you hear that?

ANOTHER.   Really, what can one say?

ANOTHER. Dear Lord in heaven!

CYRANO (*gallantly*). Ladies of rank and beauty,
Shiners, enchanters, take it as your duty
To inspire a poem or epigrammatic witticism,
But keep your pretty paws off dramatic criticism.

BELLEROSE. How about all the cash we have to give back?

CYRANO. Bellerose puts us all right. Yes, money matters.
Let it never be said that Bergerac

Wished to see Thespis's robe grow full of tatters.

He detaches a moneybag from his waist and throws it onto the stage.

Take that. Take off.

JODELET (*picking up the bag*).
                    If you'll guarantee a sack
Of loot like this, I'm ready to guarantee
To let you shut the theatre every night.

SPECTATORS. Boo. Boo. Boo.

JODELET.   Even if we
Get hissed and booed for it.

BELLEROSE.   All right, all right,
Let's clear the hall.

     But nobody wants to leave.

LE BRET. It's mad.

CITIZEN.   Yes, mad.
    (*To* CYRANO)   That very famous actor
Has His Grace the Duke of Candale as protector.
Do you have a patron?

CYRANO.   No.

CITIZEN.   No patron?

CYRANO.   No.

CITIZEN. No patron to protect you with his name?

CYRANO. No for the third time. I'm protected just the
    same.
    He taps his sword.
    This is my patroness.

CITIZEN'S SON.   You'll have to go.
You can't stay here in Paris.

CYRANO.   No?

CITIZEN.   Great God,
His Grace – don't you know how long an arm
The duke possesses?

CYRANO.   Less long than mine
  When I've screwed on this steel extension rod.
CITIZEN. You honestly think you're able to do him harm?
CYRANO. It's possible. As for you, please turn your toes
  The other way.
CITIZEN.   I beg your –
CYRANO.   Left incline,
  Or right. And, thus reorientated, walk.
  Or tell me why you're looking at my nose.

There is now a terrible expectant silence.

CITIZEN. Really, I –
CYRANO.   Unusual, is it? Come on, talk,
  Talker, tell me all about it.
CITIZEN.   Really, I
  Try not to look at your nose, sir, really –
CYRANO.   Why?
  Does it disgust you?
CITIZEN.   No, no, not at all.
CYRANO. Too lurid, is it? Oversized?
CITIZEN.   It's small,
  Beautifully small. It's minute – minuscule.
CYRANO. Compound your insolence with ridicule,
  Would you? My nose is small, eh, *small*?
CITIZEN.   Oh God –
CYRANO. My nose, sir, is enormous. Ignorant clod,
  Cretinous moron, a man ought to be proud,
  Yes, proud, of having so proud an appendix
  Of flesh and bone to crown his countenance,
  Provided a great nose may be an index
  Of a great soul – affable, kind, endowed
  With wit and liberality and courage
  And courtesy – like mine, you rat-brained dunce,
  And not like yours, a cup of rancid porridge.
  As for your wretched mug – all that it shows

Is lack of fire, spunk, spark, of genius, pride,
Lack of the lyrical and picturesque,
Of moral probity – in brief, of nose.
To fist such nothingness would be grotesque,
So take a boot instead on your backside.

He kicks him. Whimpering, the CITIZEN *leaves, his* SON,
not too displeased, after him. The aristocrats react unfavourably.

DE GUICHE. He's a bit of a bore.
VALVERT. A braggart.
DE GUICHE. Who shall it be,
My lords?
VALVERT (*standing up*).
In very bad taste. Only a pig
Of a plebeian would sprout a snout like that.
DE GUICHE. So may we
Leave it to you?
VALVERT. Yes, you can leave it to me.

So saying, he approaches CYRANO *with a sneer of great insolence.*

That thing of yours is big, what? Very big.
CYRANO (*most affably*).
Precisely what I was saying.
VALVERT. Ha!
CYRANO. Nothing more?
Just a fatuous smirk? Oh, come, there are fifty=score
Varieties of comment you could find
If you possessed a modicum of mind.
For instance, there's the frank aggressive kind:
'If mine achieved that hypertrophic state,
I'd call a surgeon in to amputate.'
The friendly: 'It must dip into your cup.
You need a nasal crane to hoist it up.'

The pure descriptive: 'From its size and shape,
I'd say it was a rock, a bluff, a cape –
No, a peninsula – how picturesque!'
The curious: 'What's that? A writing desk?'
The gracious: 'Are you fond of birds? How sweet –
A Gothic perch to rest their tiny feet.'
The truculent: 'You a smoker? I suppose
The fumes must gush out fiercely from that nose
And people think a chimney is on fire.'
Considerate: 'It will drag you in the mire
Head first, the weight that's concentrated there.
Walk carefully.' The tender-hearted swear
They'll have a miniature umbrella made
To keep the rain off; or for summer shade.
Then comes the pedant: 'Let me see it, please.
That mythic beast of Aristophanes,
The hippocampocamelelephunt,
Had flesh and bone like that stuck up in front.'
Insolent: 'Quite a useful gadget, that.
You hold it high and then hang up your hat.'
Emphatic: 'No fierce wind from near or far,
Save the mistral, could give that nose catarrh.'
Impressed: 'A sign for a perfumery!'
Dramatic: 'When it bleeds, it's the Red Sea.'
Lyric: 'Ah, Triton rising from the waters,
Honking his wreathed conch at Neptune's daughters.'
Naïve: 'How much to view the monument?'
Speculative: 'Tell me, what's the rent
For each or both of those unfurnished flats?'
Rustic: 'Nay, Jarge, that ain't no nose. Why, that's
A giant turnip or a midget marrow.
Let's dig it up and load it on the barrow.'
The warlike: 'Train it on the enemy!'
Practical: 'Put that in a lottery
For noses, and it's bound to win first prize.'

And finally, with tragic cries and sighs,
The language finely wrought and deeply felt:
'Oh that this too too solid nose would melt.'
That is the sort of thing you could have said
If you, Sir Moron, were a man of letters
Or had an ounce of spunk inside your head.
But you've no letters, have you, save the three
Required for self-description: S.O.T.
You have to leave my worsting to your betters,
Or better, who can best you, meaning me.
But be quite sure, you lesser feathered tit,
Even if you possessed the words and wit,
I'd never let you get away with it.

DE GUICHE (*apprehensive now*).
Come away, viscount, leave him.

VALVERT (*suffocating with rage*).

Arrogant, base
Nonentity, without even a pair of gloves
To his name, let alone the ribbons and lace
And velvet that a man of breeding loves.

CYRANO. I'm one of those who wear their elegance
Within. To strut around and dance and prance
Got up like a dog's dinner – that's not me.
Less of a fop than you, sir, I may be,
But I'm more wholesome. I have never wandered
Abroad without my insults freshly laundered,
Or conscience with the sleep picked from its eye,
Or honour with unragged cuffs. Why, my
Very scruples get a manicure.
When I walk out I like to be quite sure
I smell of nothing but scrubbed liberty
And polished independence. You will see
My soul a ramrod as if corseted
And as for ribbons, all I ever did
Brave and adventurous flutters from my clothes.

With spirits high, twirled like mustachios,
Among the false and mean I walk about,
And as for spurs, I let the truth clash out.
VALVERT (*spluttering*). You —
CYRANO.   Gloves, you mentioned
  gloves. You have me there.
  I have this one left over from a pair —

> *He produces it from his pocket, and a wretched ragged
> fingerless thing it is.*

An old, old pair. Its fellow I can't trace.
I think I left it in some viscount's face.
VALVERT (*throbbing with rage*).
  Cad, villain, clod, flatfooted bloody fool!

> CYRANO, *unmoved, doffs his hat and bows low.*

CYRANO. And *I'm* Cyrano Savinien-Hercule
  De Bergerac.

> VALVERT *gives him the mandatory glove-blow — on his
> nose.* CYRANO *remains unmoved.*

VALVERT.   There.
CYRANO.   Would you be terribly bored
  If I composed a poem?
VALVERT (*sneering*).   Poet, eh?
CYRANO.   My lord,
  I'm thoroughly versed in churning verses out
  Even while rattling ironware about.
  I'll improvise a ballade.
VALVERT (*sneering still*).
                              A ballade.
CYRANO. Sorry, my lord, to baffle you with hard
  Technical expressions. I'll explain.
  Three eight-lined stanzas and then one quatrain,
  The envoy. Sir, thus my proposal goes:

To fight and at the same time to compose
A ballade of strict classical design,
And then to kill you on the final line.
VALVERT (*sure of himself*).
Oh, no.
CYRANO.   No? 'Ballade of a Fencing Bout
Between de Bergerac and a Foppish Lout.'
VALVERT (*drawing his sword*).
Well, when you've finished your doggerel recital –
CYRANO (*kindly*).
That was no doggerel. That was the title.
Wait. Let me choose my rhymes –
VALVERT.   Ape.
CYRANO.   That's one.
RAGUENEAU.   Eel.
CYRANO. Thank you. Ape rape grape shape feel meal deal
     seal.
I'm ready.

> *The fighting ballade begins, with* CYRANO *suiting action to
> words all through it.*

> I bare my head from crown to nape
> And slowly, leisurely reveal
> The fighting trim beneath my cape,
> Then finally I strip my steel.
> A thoroughbred from head to heel,
> Disdainful of the rein or bit,
> Tonight I draw a lyric wheel,
> But, when the poem ends, I hit.

> Come and be burst, you purple grape,
> Spurt out the juice beneath your peel.
> Gibber, and show, you ribboned ape,
> The fat your folderols conceal.
> Let's ring your bells – a pretty peal!

Is that a fly? I'll see to it.
Ah, soon you'll feel your blood congeal,
For, when the poem ends, I hit.

I need a rhyme to hold the shape –
Gape, fish. I'm going to wind the reel.
My rod is lusting for its rape,
This sharp tooth slavers for its meal.
There, let it strike. Ah, did you feel
The bite? Not yet. The vultures sit
Until the closing of the deal.
The poem ends, and *then* I hit.

He stands solemnly to attention.

ENVOY.

Prince, drop your weapon. Humbly kneel,
Seek grace from God in requisite
Repentance. Now – I stamp the seal.
The poem ended – and I hit!

He dispatches the viscount neatly. VALVERT *falls, and his friends gather round him. During the following his body is carried off. There is great excitement and jubilation.*

CAVALRYMAN. Superb.
A LADY. 　　　　　　　　Exquisite.
RAGUENEAU. 　　　　　　　　Phenomenal.
LE BRET. 　　　　　　　　　　　　Quite mad.
CUIGY. Heroic.

A MUSKETEER *not previously noticed comes up to* CYRANO.
THE MUSKETEER. Sir, I should be more than glad
　If you'd accept the homage, sir, of one
　Who knows style when he sees it. Oh, *well done.*

　He goes off.

CYRANO (*to* LE BRET).
　That gentleman – who is he?

LE BRET.   D'Artagnan.
  Come on, let's talk.
CYRANO.   Wait till the mob dies down.
(*To* BELLEROSE)
May we stay here a while?
BELLEROSE.   Of course you can.

    There is much noise outside. JODELET *comes in to report.*

JODELET. He's being booted and hooted out of town,
  Montfleury.
BELLEROSE.   Tragic stilts to running sandals.
Sic transit. Lock up, but don't douse the candles.
We're rehearsing a farce for tomorrow in a
Quarter of an hour or so. First, though, dinner.

    The DOORKEEPER *goes off to do* BELLEROSE'*s bidding, but
    first he addresses* CYRANO.

DOORKEEPER. Will you want dinner?
CYRANO.   Me? No.
LE BRET.   And why
  not?
CYRANO. No money.
LE BRET.   I see. Every sou you'd got –
CYRANO.   Oh, shall we say:
    One glorious day
    Of life for a month's pay.
LE BRET. And how will you live the month out?
CYRANO.   I don't
  know.
LE BRET. A stupid act.
CYRANO.   A marvellous gesture, though.

    The FOODSELLER *has been hovering with her cart of
    comestibles.*

FOODSELLER. Pardon, sir, I couldn't help but hear.
  You mustn't starve. Take something. Please.

CYRANO.   My dear,
  The pride of a Gascon, you must understand,
  Forbids my taking from your lily hand
  The tiniest morsel. But rather than rebuff
  Such kindness – just a grape – one is enough –
  A glass of water. Half a biscuit.
LE BRET.   This
  Is stupid.
FOODSELLER. Nothing more?
CYRANO.   Your hand to kiss.

  He salutes her courteously.

FOODSELLER. Thank you, sir. Goodnight.

  She trips off queenlily. CYRANO *spreads his handkerchief on
  a bench and sits before it with a gourmet's seriousness. He
  and* LE BRET *are now quite alone.*

CYRANO.   Well now, we're
    able
  To talk at last. Dinner is on the table –
  Main course, a drink, dessert. Strangely, I find
  I've quite an appetite. What's on your mind?
LE BRET. Listen. These jingling fops with their bellicose
    airs
  Are starting to twist and torture your ideas
  Of gentlemanly behaviour. Ask anyone
  Of sense what they think of these – carryings on.
CYRANO (*eating*).
  Delicious.
LE BRET.   The cardinal –
CYRANO.   He was here?
LE BRET.   Richelieu
  Is bound to find that sort of thing –
CYRANO.   *Vieux jeu.*
LE BRET. Have some sense.

CYRANO.   He's an author himself. He
     won't rage
   To see someone else's play kicked off the stage.
LE BRET. But can't you understand? Your enemies
   Are multiplying.
CYRANO.   The latest figure is . . .?
LE BRET. Excluding women, forty-eight, by my count.
CYRANO. Enumerate.
LE BRET.   Oh, Montfleury, the viscount –
   His relicts, I mean – the author's friends, that frightful
   De Guiche, of course, the Academy –
CYRANO.   Delightful.
LE BRET. This life of yours – where will it lead you to?
   What system is it based on?
CYRANO.   Bumbling through
   In aimless complication, forced to play
   Too many parts – that was my old way.
   But now –
LE BRET.   What?
CYRANO.   I'm going to take the simplest
   Approach to life of all, simplest and best.
   Best is the word. I've decided to excel
   In everything.
LE BRET (*sighing*).
                    I let that pass. Now tell
   Me, please, the thing I really want to know –
   Your true reason, *true*, mind, for this show
   Of hate for Montfleury.
CYRANO (*with bitter detestation*).
                          That paunch, that maw,
   Too fat to scratch his navel with his paw,
   Believes he's a sweet danger to the ladies.
   Why, even when mouthing tragedy, he's made his
   Frog's eyes into sheep's eyes of fat lust.
   I've seen him, and I've choked down my disgust.

Until, one night, one victim that he chose –
Ugh, a slug slithering over a white rose –
One lady . . .
LE BRET.   Yes?
CYRANO.   I was in love with. No, God knows,
I *am* in love with –
LE BRET (*greatly surprised*).
                              But you never said one word.
How could he know, how could anyone?
CYRANO.   Absurd,
Isn't it? This nose precedes me everywhere,
A quarter of an hour in front, to say 'Beware:
Don't love Cyrano' to even the ugliest.
And Cyrano now has to love the best,
The brightest, bravest, wittiest, the most
Beautiful.
LE BRET.   Beautiful?
CYRANO.   France cannot boast,
Nor Europe, nor all territories beyond,
A girl more lissom, gossamer-fine, more blonde –
LE BRET. Blonde? My God, who is this woman?

> CYRANO, *with no deliberate intention, now falls into the pattern of a Petrarchan sonnet, as though this lady were Laura.*

CYRANO.   She's
A mortal danger without knowing it,
Undreamed-of-in-her-own-dreams exquisite,
A roseleaf ambush where love lurks to seize
The unwary heart. The unwary eye that sees
Her smile sees pearled perfection. She can knit
Grace from a twine of air. The heavens sit
In every gesture. Of divinities
She's most divine. O Venus, amorous queen,
You never stepped into your shell; Dian –

You never glided through the summer's green
As *she* steps into her chair and then is seen
Gliding through dirty Paris –
LE BRET.   There's no ban
On uttering her name – your cousin's name?
CYRANO. It rhymes, and that's enough. Let not the shame
Of the dusty air besmirch it –
LE BRET.   Oh – absurd.
This is the finest news I ever heard.
You love her? Fine – so go and tell her so.
Tonight you're covered in a golden glow
Of glory in her eyes.
CYRANO.   This – gross protuberance.
Look at it, and tell me what exuberance
Of hope can swell the rest of me. I'm under
No illusion. Oh, sometimes, bemused by the wonder
Of a blue evening, a garden of lilac and rose,
Letting this wretched devil of a nose
Breathe in the perfume, I follow with my eye –
Under that silver glory in the sky –
Some woman on the arm of a cavalier,
And dream that I too could be strolling there,
With such a girl on *my* arm, under the moon.
My heart lifts, I forget my curse, but soon,
Suddenly, I perceive what kills it all –
My profile shadowed on the garden wall.
LE BRET (*with pity*).
My friend –
CYRANO.   My friend, why should providence allot
Such ugliness, such loneliness?
LE BRET.   You're not
Crying?
CYRANO. Oh, never, never that. To see
A long tear straggling along this nose would be
Intolerably ugly. I wouldn't permit

A crystal tear fraught with such exquisite
Limpidity to be defiled by my
Gross snout. Tears are sublime things, and I,
Wedding a nymph to a rhinoceros,
Would render the sublime ridiculous.

> *But this speech, rendered rapidly and unrhetorically, is a
> kind of handkerchief.*

LE BRET. All right, not crying, but still sad. Yet love
Is an imponderable, not a matter of –
Well, nasal mensuration. March right in.
If love, as they say, is a lottery, you can –
CYRANO.   Argh.
I love Cleopatra. Have I Antony's
Glamour and glow and glory? And if she's
Hero, though I can swim, I'm no Leander.
A new Roxane needs a new Alexander,
And I'm the Great in only one respect.
Helen of Paris – whom can she select
But Paris of Paris? I'm not he.
LE BRET.   But your wit,
Your courage – they can earn love. Surely it
Was proved just now. The girl who offered you
Food – did her eyes show hate, revulsion?
CYRANO (*doubtfully*).   True.
LE BRET. Well, then – I saw her face, Roxane's, tonight
During your duel. It was ghastly white.
That skill, that courage got the girl. You're half-
Way there. Now dare to speak.
CYRANO.   So she can laugh
At *this*? Why, man, there's nothing that I fear
More in this world –

> *During the above, the* DOORKEEPER *has made a quiet
> entrance.*

DOORKEEPER. Monsieur, there's someone here
Who'd like a word with you.

They see who it is.

CYRANO. Heavens, her chaperone.

Roxane's DUENNA *comes up to them, curtsies, and speaks in prose.*

DUENNA. I have a message. My lady says she'd be glad if
her brave cousin, as she puts it, would be good enough to
meet her in private, as she puts it.

CYRANO (*astonished*). She wants to meet me?

DUENNA. She has something to say to you, so she says to
me. She's going to early mass tomorrow. Saint-Roch. She
wants to know where she can see you afterwards.

CYRANO. Oh, heavens, let me think –

DUENNA. Where?

CYRANO. I'm thinking where. Where? At the shop of
Monsieur Ragueneau the pastrycook.

DUENNA. Where?

CYRANO. At the shop of – in the rue Saint-Honoré.

DUENNA. Seven o'clock. She'll be there.

CYRANO. I'll be there.

DUENNA. I'll be with her. Goodnight.

She curtsies and is off. LE BRET *and* CYRANO *look at each
other in joy.*

CYRANO. Me – she wants to see *me*.

LE BRET. So it's goodbye
To misery?

CYRANO. Whatever she wants, it means that I
At least exist for her –

LE BRET. So now – an accession of calm?

CYRANO. Calm? With ten hearts beating within, each arm
As muscular as twenty? My arteries thud

With thunder, lightning's jagging through my blood.
I need an army meet for my defiance.
So take away your dwarfs – bring on your giants!

*During the above, the theatrical company, in commedia
dell'arte costumes, have been assembling on the stage.*

BELLEROSE. Quiet down there, we're rehearsing.
CYRANO (*laughing*).   And
    we're off.

They march towards the door, but this opens, and CUIGY
and BRISSAILLE *half carry in the dead-drunk* LIGNIÈRE.

CUIGY. Thank God you're here.
CYRANO.   What the devil –
BRISSAILLE.   Devil
    enough,
  This one.
CYRANO.   What's the trouble?

    LIGNIÈRE, *thick-voiced, tremulously proffers a tattered piece
    of paper.* CYRANO *reads what is on it.*

LIGNIÈRE.   I got this note.
  A hundred men – because of a song I wrote –
  I daren't go home – you hear – a hundred men –
  Going to get me – armed, the lot of them – when
  I go through the Porte de Nesle – my way home. Let me
  Stay in your place – hundred men – going to get me.
CYRANO (*with restrained joy*).
  A hundred men? Tonight you lay your head
  On your own pillow.
LIGNIÈRE.   But –
CYRANO.   I'll turn down your bed
  Myself. I swear it. Now, get off your knees
  And take that lantern.

    He means one of the enclosed candles used for lighting the theatre. LIGNIÈRE *shakily obeys.* CYRANO *addresses the others.*

You, the witnesses
Of what I intend to do, come too, but please
Keep a safe distance.

CUIGY.   You mean – you're going to fight
One hundred men?

CYRANO.   Certainly. Tonight
Less than a hundred would be far too few.

> The ACTORS *and* ACTRESSES, *intrigued, have come down
> from the stage.*

LE BRET (*indicating* LIGNIÈRE).
But why protect this –?

CYRANO.   I expected you,
Captain, to raise objections.

LE BRET.   Drunken sot?

CYRANO. This drunken sot, this claret butt, this pot
Of mountain dew, once did a thing as pretty
As ever I saw. It happened here, in the city.
Mass had just ended. He saw a girl he loved
Dip in the holy water font. He shoved
His whole head in and drank the blessed lot.

ACTRESS. A lovely thing to do.

CYRANO.   Yes, was it not?
Sot!

> *He tousles* LIGNIÈRE's *hair affectionately and claps a hat on it.*

ACTRESS. But a hundred men against one poor
Poet – why?

CYRANO.   Let's march. When I make for
The enemy, don't help, no matter what
The danger.

ANOTHER ACTRESS. I must come and see.

CYRANO.   Why not?
All of you? Make with mad and motley charm a

Blend of Italian farce and Spanish drama.
Bring silver music, so the noisy scene
Both thuds and jingles – like a tambourine.
ACTRESSES. Wonderful – quick, a cloak – I need a hood.
CYRANO. Gentlemen of the orchestra, will you . . . ? Good.

He starts getting his retinue in line

Gentlemen first, the ladies next, but some
Twenty paces in the van I come
Alone, save for this triple-waving plume,
This proud panache. Nobody must presume
To aid me in this fight – *my* fight, *my* war.
One, two, three – doorman, open up the door.

The DOORKEEPER *opens up the fourth wall. Nocturnal music sounds from the heavens.*

Ah, Paris, swimming through nocturnal mist,
The rooftops draped in azure, shyly kissed
By an uncertain moon – proscenium
All dressed and ready for the scene to come.
Below, threading the fog, a silver skein,
Or like a magic mirror, breathes the Seine,
Trembling, compact of myth and mystery –
You're going to see now what you're going to see.
To the Porte de Nesle!
EVERYBODY.   To the Porte de –

CYRANO *stops them with an upheld hand and answers a question already asked.*

CYRANO.   There was
A question: why do five-score enemies
Seek to stick five-score daggers in the back
Of one poor poet? Answer: it's because
They know this poor defenceless rhymer is
A friend of Cyrano de Bergerac!

To the Porte de Nesle!

EVERYBODY.   To the Porte de Nesle!

Music. Off they go.

CURTAIN

Act II

Ragueneau's shop

*It is the following morning, very early, dawn indeed.
Ragueneau's rôtisserie already exudes heartening aromas of
things aroast and abake.* RAGUENEAU *himself sits at a table
counting off poetic feet on his fingers, between two of which is a
quill pen. Scrawled paper is before him.* COOKS *emerge from the
kitchen bearing dishes which they place upon a counter. They
announce what the dishes are.*

FIRST COOK. Fruit flan.
SECOND COOK. Terrine of beef.
THIRD COOK. Pork pâté.
FOURTH COOK. Tarts.

> *Having set down their trays, they return to the kitchen.*
> RAGUENEAU *sighs.*

RAGUENEAU. Smelling hot fat, my frigid muse departs.
   The dawn is silvering each casserole,
   So lock the god of poetry in your soul.
   Quit cool Parnassus for this nether fire.
   The ovens beckon. *Au revoir*, my lyre.

> *Some of the baking and roasting proceeds in the back part of
> the shop itself.* RAGUENEAU *superintends the work. He
> addresses a baker.*

These lumps are badly placed. You have to fix
The caesura there – between the hemistichs.
(*To one working on a piecrust*)
This dome of pastry needs a cupola.
(*To one who is fixing poultry on spits*)
You – alternate the modest fowl and the
Proud turkey like the long verse and the short.
Thus you compose upon the spit a sort
Of browning stanza, a roast symmetry.

> *An* APPRENTICE *brings in a pastry confection in the shape of a lyre.* RAGUENEAU *is deeply touched.*

APPRENTICE. How do you like it, sir?
RAGUENEAU.   You thought of me.
Charming.
APPRENTICE. *Brioche.* The strings here are a little –
RAGUENEAU. Brittle?
APPRENTICE.   Sugar.
RAGUENEAU.   At last a synthesis
Of poetry and pastry. Good. Drink this.

> *He gives the* APPRENTICE *money. But* LISE, *Ragueneau's wife, comes in. She carries paper bags to give him. On her feet shoe-dusters are affixed for polishing the floor. She is prettyish, dumpy, flirtatious, a shrew.*

Here comes your mistress. Hide the money, quick.
(*Ingratiatingly*)
How do you like it, dear – this thing?
LISE.   Ridic-
Ulous.
RAGUENEAU. Ulous. Paper bags? Good. Good
God, woman, this is poetry – how could
You desecrate – dismember my friends' verse?
Blasphemy, sacrilege – ah, no, it's worse –
It's the Bacchantes ripping Orpheus again.

LISE. What else are those rotten scribbles fit for, then?
    They'll do a job now, and that's fit and proper.
RAGUENEAU (*weightily*).
    Ant – you're insulting the divine grasshopper.
LISE. A rotten lot – all ragged shirts and pants –
    Before you met them you never called me ants
    And back ants.
RAGUENEAU.   But – to do *that*, with *those*!
    It makes me wonder what you'd do with prose.

> *Scratching his bottom, shaking his head, he goes towards the*
> *counter. Two* CHILDREN *enter.*

RAGUENEAU. Yes, my pretties?
FIRST CHILD.   Three pies.
RAGUENEAU.   How about these –
    All hot and brown?
SECOND CHILD.   Please will you wrap them, please?
RAGUENEAU. Ah God, my poets' poems. Heavens, this is
    Penelope's epistle to Ulysses.
    Not that. 'The god Apollo, blond and bright . . .'
    Not that one either.
LISE (*pausing in her dusting*).
                          Don't keep the customers waiting.
RAGUENEAU. 'Sonnet to Phyllis' – sacrilege. Oh, all right.

> *She turns her back. He addresses the* CHILDREN *earnestly in*
> *a whisper.*

Don't go away. Come back. Here – give it me,
And I'll let you have six pies instead of three.

> *The* CHILDREN *happily run off with six pies unwrapped.*
> RAGUENEAU *unhappily smooths out the defiled poem.*

RAGUENEAU. 'O glorious Phyllis' – what an inglorious
    shame:
    Some cooking fat has smeared that lovely name.

CYRANO *enters impetuously*.

CYRANO. What time is it?

RAGUENEAU. Six o'clock.

CYRANO. Another hour.

RAGUENEAU *(coming towards him)*.
Felicitations. Ah – such skill, such power.
I saw it all.

CYRANO. Saw what all?

RAGUENEAU. Your duel in rhyme.

LISE. He talks about it all the blessed time.

CYRANO. Oh, that –

RAGUENEAU. 'The poem ended – and I hit.'
Such a synthesis of steel and style – such tricks,
Such tropes –

CYRANO. The time?

RAGUENEAU. Thirty seconds past six.

LISE *comes towards him in her dusting dance and, with woman's sharpness, sees that he has a slash on his hand.*

Rhyme and rapier – wonderful. 'The poem ended –
And I –

LISE. Ah, shut up. Here you – where and when did
You get that?

CYRANO. Only a scratch.

LISE. Patch it, get some ointment.

CYRANO. It's nothing, I tell you. Listen, I have an
appointment
Here, soon. Leave us alone, will you?

RAGUENEAU. Alone? I can't. You see, my poets are due –

LISE. That's right. For their first meal of the day.

CYRANO. When I give you the signal, get them away.
The time?

RAGUENEAU. Six and ninety seconds.

CYRANO. – To write it on.
Ah.

He sits at Ragueneau's table. He examines a poetic draft and winces. He takes a clean sheet of paper. He looks for a pen. RAGUENEAU *gives him one from behind his ear.*

RAGUENEAU. Try this. It once belonged to a swan.

> CYRANO *nods his thanks and takes it. He prepares to write.. The* MUSKETEER *we saw at the theatre comes in loudly and confidently. He goes straight to* LISE.

MUSKETEER. Morning!

CYRANO. What's that?

RAGUENEAU (*resignedly*). A sort of friend of my wife.
Very fierce. So he tells me.

CYRANO. Right. Write.
Fold. Give it her. Transform my life.
The time?

RAGUENEAU. Two minutes past.

CYRANO. Of all within
I have of words, just one. Oh, let's begin.
Letter written a hundred times in my heart –
It's ready enough. Why hesitate to start?
My soul on paper – hope unmarked by doubt.
A simple matter of copying it out.

> *He writes. Ragueneau's* POET FRIENDS, *having cast their wretched shadows on the window, come in, filthy, ragged, probably untalented. There are five of them.*

LISE. Here comes the gorgers.

> *They ignore* LISE *and greet* RAGUENEAU *extravagantly.*

FIRST POET. *Confrère!*

SECOND POET. *Cher confrère!*

THIRD POET. Lord of the heavenly roast.

FOURTH POET (*sniffing*) How good the air
Smells in thy dwelling.

FIFTH POET. Phoebus of the flans.

FIRST POET. Apollo of the *poulet*.

RAGUENEAU.   They make a man's
Heart lift on very entrance.

*They start eating, but only behind each other's backs. They
have a certain rough delicacy.*

FIRST POET.   Sorry we're late.
We got held up by the crowd at the Porte de Nesle.

SECOND POET. Villainous-looking corpses head to tail
Laid in the morning mud. I counted eight.

CYRANO (*without looking up*).
I made it seven.

RAGUENEAU (*to* CYRANO).
             Do you happen to know
Who the hero of this massacre happens to be?

CYRANO (*writing*). Me? No?

THIRD POET.   He split from the nave to the
chaps
These eight – or seven – and sent off ninety-three –
Or two – screaming like cats.

LISE (*to the* MUSKETEER).   Do *you* know?

MUSKETEER (*twirling his moustache*).   Perhaps.

CYRANO (*writing*). *Je vous aime . . .*

SECOND POET.   Blood guts brains
swords pikes –

CYRANO.   *Vos yeux . . .*

FIRST POET. Hats and cloaks as far as the Quai des Orfèvres –

SECOND POET. He must have been the devil himself –

CYRANO.   *Vos
lèvres.*

THIRD POET. A giant, a monster, without one particle of—

CYRANO. 'Fear makes me tremble when I look at you.'

FOURTH POET. Written any poems lately, Ragueneau?

CYRANO (*finishing his letter*).
                          That
will do.

No signature. End, as begin, with love.
Then give it to her –
RAGUENEAU.   I've done this little thing –
A recipe in verse.

The POETS, *anticipating their reward for listening, fall to*
more openly.

FIRST POET (*munching*).
                    We're all ears.
SECOND POET (*indistinctly*).
                                        Sing.
THIRD POET. Feed us, I mean Phoebus, flash lyric fire.

POETS 4 *and* 5 *are now working, from opposite ends, on the*
lyre-shaped confectionary.

FOURTH POET. For the first time in history, the lyre
Sustains the poet.
FIRST POET (*to* SECOND POET).
                    Having a good breakfast?
SECOND POET.   Dinner
Of the night before last.
RAGUENEAU.   Gentlemen, I'll begin. 'A
Recipe for Making Almond Tarts.'

The POETS *applaud as if they had already heard the poem.*
RAGUENEAU *gently rebukes them.*

That is the title. *Now* the poem starts.

Poised on steady legs,
First your poet begs
Several eggs.
Froth them to a mousse,
And then introduce
Lemon juice.
Shimmering like silk,

Aromatic milk
Of almonds will c-
ome next, and next prepare
Pastry light as air
To coat with care
Each pretty pastry mould,
Which sweetly will enfold
The liquid gold.
Smile, a father, fond.
Wave your fiery wand,
Bake till blond.
Melting mouths and hearts,
Mmmmmm, saliva starts –
Almond tarts.

POETS. Exquisite! Delicious!

FIRST POET (*belching*).

Waaaaargh.

CYRANO. That ninth line's
rough.

RAGUENEAU, *counting on his fingers, nods ruefully.*

RAGUENEAU. Will c – ome.

CYRANO. Don't you see how they stuff
and stuff?

RAGUENEAU. They're welc – ome. Yes, I see it well enough,
But I don't look. Looking would put them off.
Don't worry about me. I get a double treat:
They listen, but, better than that, they eat.
They need to.

CYRANO (*affectionately punching him*).

You're a good man, Ragueneau.

RAGUENEAU *talks with his friends about prosody.* CYRANO
goes over to LISE, *who leaves her* MUSKETEER *to go over to
him.*

Madame, a word.
LISE (*truculently*).   What about?
CYRANO.   Keep it low.
Tell me, is he laying siege, this musketeer?
LISE. Nobody goes too far with me. All I do
Is shoot them down with my eyes.
CYRANO.   Indeed? Those two
Blue conquerors look strangely conquered to me.
They're showing their white flags.
LISE.   Now you look here –
CYRANO. Your generous-hearted husband happens to be
A friend of mine. And I will not let you
Ridicule him, cuckold him, the two –
Ridicuckold –
LISE.   If you think that –
CYRANO.   I do.

He moves nearer to the MUSKETEER *and speaks more loudly.*

A word to the wise, as the saying goes,
Of – if your Latin isn't rusty too –

He indicates the MUSKETEER's *scabbarded sword.*

Verb. sap.

He marches back towards RAGUENEAU.

LISE (*enraged*).
               Give him a slap on his nose.
MUSKETEER. His nose, yes, his nose –

But CYRANO *turns and quells him with a look. The* MUSKETEER *doffs his hat and smiles ingratiatingly.*

                              Pardon me.
I was just –

But CYRANO's *look is enough to send him scuttling off to, presumably, the living quarters of the premises.* LISE, *blazing, follows him.* CYRANO *sees a couple of shadows on the window. He indicates to* RAGUENEAU *that the shop be cleared.*

CYRANO.   Psst.
RAGUENEAU (*to the* POETS).
            Let's go inside. It will be
Less distracting – for the Muse, that is.
FIRST POET (*with rare candour*).
To hell with the Muse. Food first.
SECOND POET (*shocked*).
                        Blasphemies.

But he is the first to take a tray of cakes and to follow RAGUENEAU. CYRANO *is alone.*

CYRANO. So out this letter comes if I can see
The faintest wisp of hope –

ROXANE, *masked, enters with her* DUENNA. *To the latter* CYRANO *at once addresses himself.*

                    Madame, a quick
Word –
DUENNA. Two if you like, monsieur.
CYRANO.   Are you
By way of being a gourmande?
DUENNA.   I can do
The gormandizing act until I'm sick.
CYRANO. Good. I take a Pindaric ode or two –
DUENNA. Eh?
CYRANO.   Making the subject-matter chocolate éclairs.

He suits actions to words.

DUENNA. Ah!
CYRANO.   Do you like cream puffs?
DUENNA.   So long as there's
More cream than puff.

CYRANO.   This ode looks puffy enough.
  As for this epic on a lovesick soul –
  It's deep enough, I think, for a whole jam roll.
  Go and commune, madame, with the rising sun.
  Masticate thoroughly. Don't come back till you're
      done.

> *The* DUENNA *is not sure whether she is doing the right
> thing. Greed defeats duty. She goes out cake-laden.*
> CYRANO *and* ROXANE *are alone.*

CYRANO. May that one hour of all the hours be blessed
  When you at last remembered I exist
  And came to tell me – what?
ROXANE.   First I must
  Thank you for last night. That wretch – that fop
  You – punctured – his patron is eaten up
  With what he calls love –
CYRANO.   De Guiche?
ROXANE.   De Guiche
      proposed
  That I should marry –
CYRANO.   A blasphemous disguise
  For his own – I see. That's one bad chapter closed.
  I fought not for my nose but your bright eyes.
ROXANE. The other thing is – I daren't mention it yet.
  I must see you first as you were – the – almost brother
  You used to be when we were children together
  Playing in the park, by the lake –
CYRANO.   How can I forget
  The summers that you spent at Bergerac?
ROXANE. When your swords were bulrushes.
CYRANO.   And the
      golden hair
  Of your doll was cornsilk.
ROXANE.   Beanfields in the air,

Green plums and perpetual playtime.

CYRANO.   Puppies and
   Mulberries. Heavens, how I'm taken back.

ROXANE. To when my wish was always your command.

CYRANO. Short-skirted Roxane. You used to be
   Madeleine.

ROXANE. Was I pretty?

CYRANO.   You were never exactly plain.

ROXANE. I remember – you'd climb a tree and hurt your
   hand,
   And come running to me. And then I'd play
   The mother, and all gruff and grown-up I'd say:
   'How on earth did you manage to –?'

   *She has taken his hand. That scratch looks more serious
   than* CYRANO *said. He tries to snatch it away but she grasps
   it firmly.*

                                        Oh, no. How
   On earth? Let me see it. *Let me see –* Oh, even now,
   At your age!

CYRANO.   A bit of rather rough play
   With some of the big boys, down by the Porte de Nesle.

ROXANE. Give it to me.

   *She dips her handkerchief in a jug of something – probably
   wine. She cleans the wound.*

CYRANO.   Yes, mama.

ROXANE.   Playing, indeed. Tell
   Me – how many of these big boys were there?

CYRANO.   Oh, about
   A hundred.

   She does not at first take this in.

ROXANE.   About a hundred. *A hundred!* Out
   With your story – come now –

CYRANO.   Out with yours –
  If it *is* a story. If you dare tell it – yet.
ROXANE. I do dare. How easily one conjures
  The scent of the past. I'm breathing it,
  And you and I are home again. So listen now.
  I'm in love with someone.
CYRANO.   Ah.
ROXANE.   With someone who
  Doesn't know, doesn't suspect.
CYRANO.   Ah.
ROXANE.   Not yet, anyway.
CYRANO. Ah.
ROXANE.   But he will know. Soon.
CYRANO.   Ah.
ROXANE.   He loves me too,
  But so far from a distance, timidly,
  Poor boy, too scared to speak.
CYRANO.   Ah.
ROXANE.   Can you say
  Nothing but 'Ah'?
CYRANO.   Ah.
ROXANE.   Give me back your hand.
  How hot it is – feverish. But I see
  Love trembling on his lip.
CYRANO.   Ah.
ROXANE.   He's a soldier, and,
  More than that, he's in your regiment.
CYRANO. Ah.
ROXANE.   More than that, even, he's in your company.
CYRANO. Ah.
ROXANE.   And such a man – intelligent,
  Young, proud, brave, beautiful.
CYRANO (*pale, rising*).   Beautiful?
ROXANE. Whatever's the matter?
CYRANO.   Nothing. Just this fool

Of a scratch I got from the big boys.

He smiles.

ROXANE.   Anyway,
   I love him. All that remains for me to say
   Is that I've only seen him at the theatre.
CYRANO.   Never met?
   Never spoken?
ROXANE.   Only with our eyes.
CYRANO.   Then how can you
   Know?
ROXANE. Oh, you know how it is. People talk –
   In the Place Royale – gossip as they walk
   Under the lime trees.
CYRANO.   He's in the Guards, you say.
   His name?
ROXANE.   Baron Christian de Neuvillette.
CYRANO. He's not in the Guards.
ROXANE.   Oh yes, he is, as from
       today –
   Under Captain Carbon de Castel-Jaloux.
CYRANO. So soon, so fast, the knife can pierce our hearts.
   My poor dear child –

   Roxane's DUENNA *comes blithely in.*

DUENNA.   Monsieur de Bergerac,
   I've eaten every single one of those tarts.
CYRANO. Good. Now read the wrappers, front and back.

   She goes out again, shrugging.

   My dear sweet child – think – consider – you
   Who love fine words, eloquence, elegance –
   He may be a fool, a savage –
ROXANE.   Oh, but his
   Curls are the curls of a Greek god.

CYRANO.   There's a chance
  That his brains may be curly too.
ROXANE.   That can't be true.
  My woman's instincts tell me otherwise.
CYRANO. Those instincts often tell the biggest lies.
  Suppose he's a boor, a bore – what will you do?
ROXANE (*with touching simplicity*).
  Well, then, I suppose I shall have to die.
CYRANO. And so – you brought me here to tell me this.
  Perhaps you'd be good enough to tell me why.
ROXANE. Yesterday someone said – oh, it frightens me –
  Somebody said that all your company
  Are Gascons.
CYRANO.   Yes, all Gascons. Ah, I see!
  It's a matter of our fiery Gascon pride
  To rip up any greenhorn from outside
  Who gets inside. Is that what you heard?
ROXANE.   I'm scared
  For him.
CYRANO (*between his teeth*).
        Not without cause.
ROXANE.   But you, who dared
  So much last night – that brute, those brutes – everyone
  Is so scared of you – I thought –
CYRANO.   Your Christian
  Shall not be thrown to the lions.
ROXANE.   For our friendship's
    sake
  You'll protect him? Defend him? You'll make
  Him your friend?
CYRANO.   There's nothing finer than
  Friendship.
ROXANE.   Promise.
CYRANO.   I promise.
ROXANE.   Don't let anyone

Fight duels with him.

CYRANO. God forbid.

ROXANE (*fervently*). Oh, Cyrano,
I love you. Tell me everything about last night
Some time, won't you? Now I have to go.
Oh, how I love you. Oh, and tell him to write.

CYRANO. Yes, yes.

ROXANE. Don't forget now. Just think – a
hundred men
Against my boy of the bulrush sword. Ah, when
There's time you must tell me. We're friends, aren't we?

CYRANO. Yes, yes.

ROXANE. Tell him to write. You and a hundred
men.
Such courage.

Leaving, she blows him a kiss. He stands frozen.

CYRANO. $>$ I've done better than that since then.

Silence. The door opens. Captain CARBON DE CASTEL-
JALOUX *comes in, a handsome, brave, rather conventional
officer.*

CARBON. May I come in?

CYRANO. Yes, yes, you love me.

CARBON. *Eh?*

CYRANO *comes to.*

CYRANO. Captain.

CARBON (*patting him on the back*).
We've heard the story, but we want it
from you.
There are thirty cadets of the Guards all ready to
Get you drunk, in the tavern across the way.
Come on.

CYRANO. I'd rather not.

CARBON *shrugs and goes to the door. He shouts. At the same time* RAGUENEAU *comes in from the kitchen.*

CARBON.   Hey there! Hey!
 Our hero's suffering from a sort of crapula –
 Too much blood. Come over.

 He strides back to CYRANO, *smiling.*

        Talk about popular –

 The CADETS *enter noisily. They express delight, in the Gascon dialect, at seeing* CYRANO.

CADETS. *Mille dioux! Capdedious! Mordious! Pocapdedious!*
RAGUENEAU. You're Gascons, gentlemen, are you – all of
 you?
FIRST CADET. Well done.
CYRANO (*formally*). Baron.
        First class.
SECOND CADET.   Baron.
CYRANO.   Bravo!
THIRD CADET.
CYRANO. Baron.
FOURTH CADET. Let me kiss you.
FIFTH CADET.   Me too.
CYRANO.   Barons – no!
RAGUENEAU. And you're all barons too?
FIRST CADET.   Baronially born.
 You could build a tower with our coronets, monsieur.
SECOND CADET. But first you'd have to get them out of
 pawn.

 During the above LE BRET *enters. He strides up to his friend.*

LE BRET. Cyrano, the whole of Paris is here,
 Looking for you – a delirious crowd behind me,
 Led by the ones you led along last night.

CYRANO. I trust you didn't say where they could find me.
LE BRET. I did.

A CITIZEN *comes in and leaves the door open.*

CITIZEN. See – carriages – the street's packed tight.
LE BRET. How about Roxane?
CYRANO. Quiet!

A crowd comes in, jubilant.

CROWD. Cyrano!
RAGUENEAU (*with delight*). My shop
Is invaded. They'll smash everything up.
Magnificent!

Members of the crowd fawn on CYRANO, *maul him, seek to embrace him.*

CROWD. My friend – my friend – my friend –
CYRANO. I never knew
I had so many friends.
LE BRET. Success at last.

CYRANO *looks bitterly at him. A foppish* MARQUIS *comes up and tries to embrace the hero.*

MARQUIS. My dear –
CYRANO. Too dear for customers like you
To handle.

He is unhandled. The MARQUIS *is affronted, but another one comes up to* CYRANO *with large enthusiasm, handling him.*

OTHER MARQUIS.
The ladies in my carriage, sir, have just
Expressed a desire to meet you. Allow me to
Present you to them.

He goes ahead, confident that CYRANO *will follow.*

CYRANO.   Certainly.
But first, sir, who'll present *you* to *me*?
LE BRET. What the –

A self-important MAN OF LETTERS *enters.*

CYRANO.   Quiet!
MAN OF LETTERS.   I'd like some details –
CYRANO.   No!
LE BRET. Oh, come now, this is Théophraste Renaudot,
Founder of the *Gazette*. Up-to-the-minute
News is his line. There's a big future in it,
Or so they tell me.

RENAUDOT *retires hurt. His place is taken by a* POET – *a
decently dressed one, not one of Ragueneau's wretched
friends.*

POET.   I'd like your permission,
Sir, to write a celebratory composition –
An acrostic on your name.
CYRANO.   I'll do it better.
I'll do it now. You can call out each letter
And I can do the rest. Come on, then – go!
POET. See –
CYRANO.   these vassals of emotion.
POET. Why –
CYRANO.   do you suppose they're there?
POET. Are –
CYRANO.   they come to bring devotion,
POET. Eh?
CYRANO. Or see a talking bear?
POET. En –
CYRANO.   y monster, sirs, will do. But
POET. Oh –
CYRANO.   the real monster's you.

He indicates the crowd around him. Nobody applauds.
There is puzzlement: why is he behaving like this? DE
GUICHE *comes in with* CUIGY, BRISSAILLE *and other*
gentlemen.

CUIGY. Monsieur de Guiche, with a message from the
    Marshal —

DE GUICHE (*taking a chair*).
  — Who wishes to convey his necessarily impartial
  Felicitations on your flamboyant bravery.

CROWD. Bravo!

CYRANO.   I respect his judgement.

DE GUICHE.   He
  Was incredulous, until the testimony
  Of these gentlemen convinced him

CUIGY.   After all, we
  Saw everything.

LE BRET (*softly, to Cyrano*).
            What's the matter?

CYRANO.   Quiet, Le Bret!

LE BRET. You look as though you're suffering. What did
    she s —

CYRANO. No!

DE GUICHE.   This incident at the Porte de Nesle
  Is, I hear, one of many — notorious,
  Glorious — I'm told it's not easy to tell.
  You're one of these wild Gascons?

CYRANO.   That is so.

DE GUICHE. These hairy, head-high heroes —

FIRST CADET.   One of us.

DE GUICHE. So these are the famous, infamous —

CARBON.   Cyrano,
  Present them.

CYRANO.   I obey your order.

CARBON.   Go!

CYRANO. These are the Gascony cadets –
         Captain Castel-Jaloux's their chief –
         Braggers of brags, layers of bets,
         They are the Gascony cadets.
         Barons who scorn mere baronets,
         Their lines are long and tempers brief –
         They are the Gascony cadets,
         With Castel-Jaloux as their chief.
         They're lithe as cats or marmosets,
         But never cherish the belief
         They can be stroked like household pets
         Or fed on what a lapdog gets.
         Their hats are fopped up with aigrettes
         Because the fabric's come to grief.
         These are the Gascony cadets.
         They scorn the scented handkerchief,
         They dance no jigs or minuets.
         They cook their enemies on brochettes,
         With blood as their apéritif.
         These are the Gascony cadets,
         Compact of brain and blood and beef,
         Contracting pregnancies and debts
         With equal lack of black regrets.
         Cuckolds, cuckoo, and cry 'Stop, thief!'
         Too late. Await the bassinets.
         Castel-Jaloux there is the chief
         Of these – the Gascony cadets.

DE GUICHE (*mildly impressed*).
    It's fashionable for a gentleman's retinue
    To contain a poet or so, so how would you
    Like to join mine?
CYRANO.   I don't like retinues.
DE GUICHE. Your performance in the theatre managed to amuse
    My uncle, Cardinal Richelieu. you know, I could,

If you cooperated, do you a little good
In that direction. I suppose, like everyone,
You've written a play in verse?

LE BRET.   Your *Agrippina* –
Here's your chance to get the thing put on.

DE GUICHE. Take it to him.

CYRANO (*half tempted*).   Hm.
                              He's expert in the drama

DE GUICHE.
Himself. Just let him, you know, reshape a scene, a
Character. He'll be happy to rewrite
The odd line here, the odd line there.

CYRANO.   I might,
If I thought of anyone's changing a single comma
Didn't make my blood curdle –

DE GUICHE.   But when he likes a
Thing he pays munificently.

CYRANO.   The golden ring
Of my own writing, lines that soar and sing
Through my brain and bones and blood, is my best
reward.

DE GUICHE. You're proud, sir – dangerously so.

CYRANO. Dangerous to myself? I think not, my lord.
To others – well –

They look at each other in reciprocal dislike. A CADET
*comes running in with a drawn sword on which torn and
battered hats are transfixed.*

CADET.   Cyrano! Cyrano –
I say – look what we found out on the street
This morning – feathers from the fowl you put to
Flight.

CARBON. Nicely mounted, very neat,
Ready for the trophy-room.

CUIGY.   He'll be not too

Pleased with himself today, the scoundrel who
Hired the hirelings who were underneath.
BRISSAILLE. Does anyone know who it was?
DE GUICHE.   Why yes, I do.
I was – the scoundrel.

The noise of merriment ceases at once.

                                    I don't use my own teeth
For biting insolent poets. I leave it to
Hirelings to chew them up.
CYRANO.   Rather endentulous
Hirelings.
CADET (*unabashed*).
                    Cyrano, what would you like us
To do with these? Boil them, broil them, bake them?
There's plenty of grease on them.
CYRANO.   Monsieur could take
Them and return them to his friends.

*So saying, he grabs the sword and lets the hats cascade from
it at* DE GUICHE's *feet.* DE GUICHE *stands and hides his fury.*

DE GUICHE.   I want my chair!
My porters! Now! As for you, monsieur –

A VOICE IN THE STREET. The chair and porters of
    Monseigneur
Le Comte de Guiche!

    DE GUICHE's *temper is under control. He speaks to* CYRANO
    almost amiably.

DE GUICHE.   Monsieur, have you read *Don
    Quixote?*
CYRANO. Read it? I've practically lived it.
DE GUICHE.   Ponder on–
PORTER. The chair is here.
DE GUICHE.   –The windmill chapter.

CYRANO. Ninety-one.

DE GUICHE. If you fight with windmills, they'll swing
their heavy spars
And spin you down to the mud.

CYRANO. Or up to the stars.

*Silence. DE GUICHE leaves. All the notables leave with him
– CUIGY and BRISSAILLE somewhat abashed – and the crowd
follows, not too happy now about calling CYRANO 'mon
ami'. The CADETS settle at a table and are eagerly served
with food and drink by RAGUENEAU. CYRANO salutes with
exaggerated courtesy those who do not dare take their leave
of him.*

CYRANO. Messieurs – messieurs – messieurs –

LE BRET. You've done
it again.

CYRANO. Stop growling.

LE BRET. No, to be quite accurate, when
A man has achieved an unprecedented ecstasy
Of excess, you can't say he's done it again.

CYRANO. I did it on principle. Excess, you see,
Is not excessive when it's been conceived
On principle. My success is achieved
Only by excess.

LE BRET. Oh, if only you'd stop
Trying to be the three musketeers and Don
Christ Quixote rolled up into one,
You'd make your way, you'd wing up to the top.

CYRANO. Up to the top. What would you have me do?
Seek out a powerful protector, pursue
A potent patron? Cling like a leeching vine
To a tree? *Crawl* my way up? Fawn, whine
For all that sticky candy called success?
No, thank you. Be a sycophant and dress
In sickly rhymes a prayer to a moneylender?

Play the buffoon, desperate to engender
A smirk on a refrigerated jowl?
No, thank you. Slake my morning mouth with foul
Lees and leavings, breakfast off a toad?
Wriggle and grovel on the dirty road
To advancement and wear the skin of my belly through?
Get grimy calluses on my kneecaps? Do
A daily dozen to soften up my spine?
No, thank you. Stroke the bristles of some swine
With one hand, feel his silk purse with the other?
Burn up the precious incense of my mother-
Wit to perfume some bad bastard's beard?
No, thank you. When all pride has disappeared,
Sail stagnant waters, with madrigals for oars,
The canvas filled with the breath of ancient whores
Or unfructified duennas? Be the pope
Of some small literary circle and softsoap
Editors and reviewers? Shall I look
For a lifetime's reputation from one book
And then give up the agonizing art
As far too wearing? No, thanks. Shall I start
Finding true genius only in imbeciles
And acneous hairy oafs? Let out shrill squeals
At being neglected by the columnists?
Live in a fog of fear, grope through the mists
Of scheming calculation? No, thanks. Is it
Best I should think it best to make a visit
Rather than make a poem? Relish the savour
Of stuffy salons? Seek condescension, favour,
Influence, introductions? No, no, no,
Thank you, no. No, thank you. But to go
Free of the filthy world, to sing, to be
Blessed with a voice vibrating virility,
Blessed with an eye equipped for looking at
Things as they really are, cocking my hat

Where I please, at a word, at a deed, at a yes or no,
Fighting or writing: this is the true life. So
I go along any road under my moon,
Careless of glory, indifferent to the boon
Or bane of fortune, without hope, without fear,
Writing only the words down that I hear
Here – and saying, with a sort of modesty,
'My heart, be satisfied with what you see
And smell and taste in your own garden – weeds,
As much as fruit and flowers.' If fate succeeds
In wresting some small triumph for me – well,
I render nothing unto Caesar, sell
No moiety of my merit to the world.
I loathe the parasite liana, curled
About the oak trunk. I myself am a tree,
Not high perhaps, not beautiful, but free –
My flesh deciduous, but the enduring bone
Of spirit tough, indifferent, and alone!
LE BRET. Alone, yes, tough, yes, but indifferent – no.
An indifferent man, God knows, doesn't go
Around as you do, seeking enemies.
CYRANO. And *you* make friends. With all deference, is
That gift not rather a canine one? You grin
At your big pack of friends, your lips tucked in
Like a hen's arse. You love new friends. I'm glad
To make new enemies.
LE BRET.   Oh, this is –
CYRANO.   Mad?
Call it my little foible. To displease
Is my chief pleasure. I love hatred. He's
My best friend who admits he's my worst foe.
You've no idea how bracing it is to go
Marching upright against a volley of venom,
In the sights of bloodshot eyes of angry men, am-
Ong the spit of bile and froth of fear,

Cooled, as by rain, by those gentle drops. My dear
Friend, you're indifferent. Who on earth could hate
   your
Guts? You're soft and warm and bland good nature,
One of these Italian cowls, comfortable, loose,
Designed for softening the chin. Now, I've no use
For anything but an iron collar, full of spikes,
Made ever spikier by new dislikes.
It makes me hold my chin up, walk erect,
A Spanish fetter blessed with the effect
Of a French halo. Hate is not a prison.
Hate is the god of day, newly arisen.
Hate is a heat that disinfects my soul.
Hate is an archangelical aureole.

LE BRET (*nodding*).
   I understand, my friend. Be bitter, proud,
   Before your foes or the indifferent crowd,
   But tell *me* that she doesn't –

CYRANO.   Not so loud.

> *He is in agony. He does not see that* CHRISTIAN *has come
> in. Shy, aware of the enmity of the south for the north, he
> sits apart from his new colleagues.*

FIRST CADET. Cyrano, tell us about it.

CYRANO.   Presently.

FIRST CADET. The story of this combat ought to be
   A good example for this new one here,
   This new-pupped, unwiped whelp, this soft-boiled egg
   That's trickled down from Normandy.

CHRISTIAN.   I beg
   Your pardon?

> *His accent becomes a subject of mockery.*

FIRST CADET.   Pardon. One word in your ear,
   Monsieur de Neuvillette. There's a subject we're

Too discreet to mention. It would be
Like talking about rope in a house where a man
Has recently hanged himself.

CHRISTIAN. What subject?

CADET. See.

He puts his hand to his nose. CYRANO, *talking with* LE
BRET, *sees and hears nothing of this exchange.*

CHRISTIAN. You mean Cyrano's?

SECOND CADET. You violate a ban
Merely by using the word. Most dangerous.
He cleft a man asunder once because
He had a cleft palate and spoke through his –

THIRD CADET. Just mention anything cartilaginous,
And – queeeek!

FIRST CADET. If you want life's chronicle to be brief,
You need do no more than take out your handkerchief.

They look solemnly at CHRISTIAN. CHRISTIAN *sees that*
CARBON *has joined* CYRANO *and* LE BRET. *He gets up and*
addresses him.

CHRISTIAN. Captain!

CARBON. Monsieur?

CHRISTIAN. What ought a man to do
When Gascons boast too much?

CARBON. He ought to show
That Normans have their share of bombast too.

CHRISTIAN. Thank you, captain. That's all I wished to
know

He goes to a chair and sits astride it like a horseman. The
CADETS *call* CYRANO.

FIRST CADET. The story!

SECOND CADET. Let's have the story!

THIRD CADET (*rather drunk*). Tell us the tale

Of what really happened at the Porte de Nesle.

FOURTH CADET (*more drunk*).

A triumph that could have been calamcalamcalamitous.

CYRANO. Very well. *My* version.

(*In hexameters*)

There, then, was the enemy. Here, then, was I,
Marching towards them. Like a great clock in the sky
The moon pulsed out at me. But suddenly I saw pass
A cottonwool cloud across it, like an angel cleaning its
      glass,
And night fell equally black on myself and my lurking
      foes —
So black that a man couldn't see even as far as his —

CHRISTIAN.   Nose.

> *There is astonishment.* CYRANO *quakes. He addresses his
> captain.*

CYRANO. Who is that man there?

CARBON.   The new man who came
  This morning.

CYRANO.   This morning

CARBON.   This morning.

CYRANO.   This
  morning.

CARBON.   His name
  is Christian de neuvi—

CYRANO (*in control*).

                        Oh, I see. Where was I?

CHRISTIAN. God knows.

CYRANO (*raging*).   *Mordious!*

> *The* CADETS *cannot at all understand his sudden restraint.*
> CYRANO *speaks naturally again.*

                        A cloud over the sky
So black a man couldn't see even as far as his toes.

And I marched along, reflecting that, to save that base
Drunken poetaster, I might be spitting in the face
Of some great man, a prince, well able to have at me
Right in the –
CHRISTIAN. Nose.
CYRANO (*controlled but sweating*).
 Teeth. But still, imprudently,
I marched. Why, though, should I stick my –
CHRISTIAN. Nose.
CYRANO. Finger in that pie?
 Was Gascon impetuosity a match for Parisian cunning?
 Could I, a Gascon, ever live down the ignominious
 running
 Of my –
CHRISTIAN. Nose?
CYRANO (*ditheringly*).
 Legs? But I said to myself: 'On, on,
 Son of Gascony, be brave, do what has to be done.
 March, Cyrano, march.' Then out of the porridge-thick
 Darkness came the first thrust, and caught me a flick –
CHRISTIAN. On the nose.
CYRANO. I parried, and found myself –
CHRISTIAN.
 Nose to nose –
CYRANO. With a hundred garlicky ruffians, from whom
 such a stink arose –
CHRISTIAN. That your nose took fright.
CYRANO. With my head
 lowered like a bull
 I charged –
CHRISTIAN. Nose to belly.
CYRANO (*desperate*). Belly of St Thomas Aquinas!

 He prepares to leap upon CHRISTIAN, *who is quite
 unperturbed.* CYRANO *controls himself with an effort and
 continues, concludes rather.*

Then I released the full
Flood of my boiling wrath. Screams of pain rang out.
Then a sword came – sneeeeeeet – and I responded –
CHRISTIAN (*high-pitched*).

                                                    Snout.

CYRANO (*furiously*).
  Out of here, everybody out of here!
FIRST CADET.   That's better.
  At last the sleeping tiger wakes again.
CYRANO. Out, out – leave me alone with this man.
SECOND CADET. Rissoles on your menu, Ragueneau.
THIRD CADET.   Get a
  Coffin ready.
RAGUENEAU.   I feel myself turning into
  A napkin.
CYRANO.   Come on, hurry it, everybody out!
FIRST CADET. What's going to happen –
SECOND CADET.   Doesn't bear
  thinking about.
THIRD CADET. The imagination –
FIRST CADET.   Positively –
SECOND CADET.   Boggles.
CYRANO.   Out,
  you.

  He kicks off the last CADET. CHRISTIAN, *standing, waits,*
  sword ready for drawing. CYRANO *then stupefies him.*

CYRANO. Come to my arms!
CHRISTIAN (*stupefied*).   Monsieur?
CYRANO.   You have courage. I
  like courage.
CHRISTIAN.   I don't think I quite –
CYRANO.   I'm her brother.
CHRISTIAN. Whose brother?
CYRANO.   Hers.

CHRISTIAN.   I don't think I quite –

CYRANO. Hers, hers.
Hers.

CHRISTIAN. Oh, my God – her brother?

CYRANO.   Near enough.
What they term a fraternal cousin.

CHRISTIAN.   And she's –
And she's – and she's –

CYRANO.   Told me everything? Yes.

CHRISTIAN. She loves – she loves – she loves me?

CYRANO.   Perhaps.

CHRISTIAN.   Oh, I'm
Overjoyed to make your acquaintance.

CYRANO.   This
Is what they call a change of heart.

CHRISTIAN.   Forgive me, please,
Forgive me.

CYRANO. You're a handsome devil, no
Doubt about that.

CHRISTIAN.   Oh, if you only knew how much
I admire you, sir.

CYRANO.   How about all those noses?

CHRISTIAN. I take them back, every single nostril.

CYRANO. Roxane expects a letter from you – tonight.

CHRISTIAN (*in deep distress*).
Oh, no.

CYRANO. What?

CHRISTIAN.   I ruin everything if I write.

CYRANO. How?

CHRISTIAN.   Because I'm such a damned fool.

CYRANO.   The way
You tackled me was not damned foolish.

CHRISTIAN.   Oh,
I can find the words when mounting an attack –
Call it military wit. But I don't know

How to mount, assault – the things to say,
I mean, when it comes to a woman. I become
Paralytic, tonguetied, speechless, dumb.
CYRANO. That's explicit enough.
CHRISTIAN.   If only I
Had the words –
CYRANO.   I have the words. All I lack
Is looks.
CHRISTIAN. You know her.
CYRANO.   Know her.
CHRISTIAN.   Know that she's so
Exquisite, sensitive – one false word and I blow
Any illusion she may have skyhigh.
CYRANO. If only I had somebody like you
As the interpreter, if I may put it so,
Of my dumb music.
CHRISTIAN.   If only I had your wit,
Your eloquence –
CYRANO.   Well, why not borrow it?
And, in return, I'll borrow your good looks.
There's promising algebra here: you plus I
Equal one hero of the story books.
CHRISTIAN. I don't think I quite –
CYRANO.   So I don't see why
I shouldn't give you words to woo her with.
CHRISTIAN. You – give – me – ?
CYRANO.   Call it a lie,
If you like, but a lie is a sort of myth
And a myth is a sort of truth. No reason why
Roxane should be disillusioned. Let's start
A fruitful collaboration.
CHRISTIAN.   You frighten me!
CYRANO. What scares you is the thought of the time when
    she
And you are alone, and you cool down her heart

With breath unwarmed by words. Well, have no fear:
My words will be with you, glued to your
Lips. What do you say?
CHRISTIAN.   I say what I said
At first: I don't quite –
CYRANO.   Understand. Unsure
About my motive? Simple: it's pure art.
The finest lines of the dramatist are dead
Without the actor's partnership. One whole
Is made from our two halves – your lips, my soul.
CHRISTIAN. I think I see. To you it's not much better
Than a refined amusement. Still, I'm grateful.
Oh God, we have to start at once –
CYRANO.   The letter.
You mean the letter.

> *He whips it out like a conjuror.*

                              Here it is, complete,
Except for the address.
CHRISTIAN.   I don't quite –
CYRANO.   It
Will serve: an exercise in poetic wit.
Poets who have no mistress but their muse
Often do this. I could serve you up a plateful
Any time. What you must do is to use
To a solid end these airy nothings. Here –
The more eloquent for being insincere.
Provide a dovecote for these harmless doves.

> CHRISTIAN *takes the letter wonderingly and handles it as if
> frightened it may go off.*

CHRISTIAN. Will these words fit her?
CYRANO.   Like a pair of gloves.
CHRISTIAN. But –
CYRANO.   She's a woman. It follows that she loves

Herself so well she's ready to believe
This is for her alone. It began with Eve,
That delusion of uniqueness.
CHRISTIAN (*sincerely grateful*).

My dear, dear –

CYRANO. Friend?

They embrace as the door opens and the CADETS *and*
RAGUENEAU *look in.* LISE *and her* MUSKETEER *appear from
the living quarters.*

FIRST CADET (*behind* RAGUENEAU *and* LE BRET).
I daren't look. The silence here –
It's a graveyard silence.
(*Seeing*)   What in the name –
SECOND CADET.   Of –
MUSKETEER (*beaming*).   Aaaah!

LE BRET (*in wonder*).
Our devil changed into a Christian brother.
Attack one nostril, and he turns the other.
MUSKETEER. And so, at last, we can talk about – haha –
Lise, come here, watch this.

He saunters insultingly up to CYRANO.

Hm, what a smell –
Wine, some rare vintage. You, with that sort of carrot,
Or shall we call it an inverted parrot
Appendage, seem equipped to sniff it well.
What is it, do you think?
CYRANO.   Oh, fresh-tapped claret.

He strikes the MUSKETEER *on the nose and sends him flying.*
LISE *is outraged,* RAGUENEAU *delighted. The rest cheer,*
patting CYRANO *on the back as they lead him out.*
CHRISTIAN *runs after, shouting.*

CHRISTIAN. Her address – you didn't give me her address!

CURTAIN

Act III

Outside Roxane's house

The house is in a little square in the old Marais. There is a garden wall with ivy and jasmine. Over the front door of the house is a balcony that gives off a tall window open to the evening air. A tall tree shades the house. There is another house near Roxane's, with a front door whose knocker is swathed to cut down noise for some reason as yet unexplained. Downstage is a stone bench. It is a glorious summer evening, but RAGUENEAU, *who sits on the bench with Roxane's* DUENNA, *does not appreciate it. He has much to moan about.*

RAGUENEAU. Ran away – absconded – just like that –
 With that damnable musketeer – leaving me flat,
 Ruined, solitary, desolate. I was ready to
 Finish things off, quit this vale of – when
  you-know-who
 Came along and offered me this position –
 Steward to madame –
DUENNA.   But how on earth did you
 Manage to get yourself into that condition?
RAGUENEAU. Oh, Lise liked men in uniform. As for me –
 Well, poets were my passion. Mars finished off
 Everything Apollo didn't scoff.
 Then Nemesis walked in, as you can see. ·

The DUENNA *nods sympathetically, then calls shrilly.*

DUENNA. Madame, are you ready? We're going to be
Late.

ROXANE (*off*).
    I'm coming.

DUENNA (*to* RAGUENEAU).
               There's this lecture on tonight
In that house there – Madame Clomire –
The Tender Passion.

RAGUENEAU (*nostalgically*).
                 Tender Passion?

DUENNA.
                        That's right.
You'd better get on with your stewardizing.

RAGUENEAU *nods sadly and gets up, walking like a broken
man into the house.* ROXANE *can be heard within.*

ROXANE. My cloak – I'm sure I left it here.

CYRANO *can be heard approaching, singing, to an accompaniment of guitar and treble recorder.*

    I praise the lilies of your skin,
      But only from afar.
    I long to venture in
      To where your roses are –

There is a discord and a cry of pain from CYRANO.

DUENNA. A bit sour.

CYRANO *appears with two musical* PAGES.

CYRANO. B natural, not B flat, you flat-headed naturals.

A PAGE. You're sure, monsieur?

CYRANO.
                    I'm sure, monsieur. A major
Chord –

ROXANE (*on the balcony*).
      Is that Cyrano?

CYRANO.   Major keys
Have major chords. Come on.
(*Sings*)
> And sipping as the bee mouth sips,
> Adore them with my lips.

ROXANE. I'm coming down.
DUENNA.   These infant prodigies –
Where did you find them?
CYRANO.   Won them in a wager
On a point of Greek grammar with the Academy.
Thank God I had them only for the day.
(*Addressing the* PAGES)
You know the house of Monsieur Montfleury?
  They shake their heads.
The fat actor?
  They nod.
                    Go to him and play
A sour serenade. Tell him, if he asks, that I'm
The donor of the treat. Play piercingly.
Play dissonantly. Play for a long time.

  The PAGES *leave.* ROXANE *appears from her front door.*
  CYRANO *bows, doffs.*

Madame, as usual, I've come to see
If our flawless friend's maintaining his sublime
Height of flight.
ROXANE.   Oh, my Christian – he
Is beautiful, brilliant – I love him desperately.
CYRANO. Brilliant?
ROXANE.   More brilliant even than you.
CYRANO (*complacently*).   I agree.
ROXANE. I've never in my life known anyone who
  Could say those little things so beautifully
  That are nothing and yet, everything. It's true
  That sometimes his muse expires into a sigh –

Inexplicably – but then she revives, and he
Says, oh he says such things –
CYRANO.   Really?
ROXANE.   You
Think, as most men think, that it's impossible
For a man to be both bright and beautiful.
CYRANO. Talks well, does he, about love and so forth?
ROXANE.   No.
  Talk is so inadequate. It's art, it's eloquence. Listen.
  'The more you take my heart, the more heart have I left,
  Dear heart, for loving you the more . . .'
CYRANO (*with an author's distaste for his own work*).
                                          Ugh.
ROXANE.   And then:
    this ache
  Of emptiness, however, bids me yearn
  To seek your heart to fill it in return.'
CYRANO. First too much and then too little. He'd
  Rhapsodize better if he'd try to learn
  To make his mind up. How much heart does he need?
ROXANE. Now you're teasing me. Jealousy, that's what it is.
CYRANO. Jealous? I?
ROXANE.   Yes, of that talent of his.
  For the last word in tenderness, listen to this:
  'Ah, in your presence, such confusion grips
  My heart that it grows wordless as a kiss.
  If kisses could but wing in wingéd words,
  Then you could read my letter with your lips.'
CYRANO. Not bad, not bad – a bit overwritten, though.
ROXANE. But listen to this –
CYRANO.   You know them off by heart?
ROXANE. All of them.
CYRANO (*twirling his moustache*).
                    Very flattering.
ROXANE.   He's so

Golden-tongued, such a master of his art.
CYRANO. Oh, I don't know – it's a sort of verbal mist,
  A rhetorical fog –
ROXANE (*stamping her foot*).
                              A master!
CYRANO (*bowing*).
                                        If you insist.

Meanwhile the DUENNA, *who has been hovering in the
garden shadows, comes running urgently towards them.*

DUENNA. Madame – Monsieur de Guiche is here. Quick,
  you,
  Monsieur Cyrano – he may put two and two
  Together if he sees you here – inside!
CYRANO (*going rapidly in*).
  Inside, inside.
ROXANE.   It's growing hard to hide
  Our secret. He'll – cut me down like a tree
  If he so much as guesses –

  DE GUICHE *comes in. He bows low.*

                              Monseigneur –

  She curtsies.

  I was just leaving.
DE GUICHE.   Alas, I'm leaving too.
  For the war.
ROXANE.   Alas.
DE GUICHE.   This very evening. We've
  Orders to besiege Arras.
ROXANE.   Arras?
DE GUICHE. Arras. Tell me, does my leaving leave
  You as cold as it seems to do?
ROXANE.   Oh, no.
DE GUICHE. I find that this present prospect of leaving you

Leaves me quite desolate. Oh, did you know
I'd been promoted colonel?
ROXANE.   Oh? Bravo.
DE GUICHE. Yes, colonel of the Guards.
ROXANE (*uneasily*).   The Guards?
DE GUICHE.   The Guards –
The regiment of that man who's big in words
And the other thing – beastly de Bergerac.
I may, with luck, get some of my own back –
ROXANE. Ordered to Arras?
DE GUICHE.   Under my command.
ROXANE. Oh, no.
DE GUICHE.   What is it?
ROXANE.   The flower in one's hand
Is so suddenly depetalled. This wind, this war
Disperses all its perfume. One loves – and then –
DE GUICHE (*eagerly*).
You've never – never spoken like this before.
You say these things – now – for the first time – when
I have to leave you –
ROXANE.   And you said, just then,
Something about revenge – my cousin –
DE GUICHE.   Ah, yes.
Are you for him?
ROXANE (*with conviction*).
                    Very much against.
DE GUICHE. You see him much?
ROXANE.   As little as I can.
DE GUICHE. I see him too much. Lately he's commenced
Keeping company with this new man –
Neuve or Neuville or something –
ROXANE.   Tall?
DE GUICHE. Tallish.
ROXANE.   Fair?

DE GUICHE.   Fairish.

ROXANE.   Handsome?

DE GUICHE.   A fool.

ROXANE. I've seen him, I think, but don't know him at all.
    To return to my cousin. Tell me what you
    Propose for Cyrano. Send him into the thick
    Of the fighting? He'll love that. I know what *I'd* do.

DE GUICHE. What?

ROXANE.   Leave him here, with his precious
      cadets,
    Kicking his heels. That ought to make him sick,
    While the rest of the regiment goes off and gets
    Medals and wounds and things. I know him. If you
    Want to strike at him – strike at his self-esteem.

DE GUICHE. Oh, woman, woman – only a woman could
    Dream up a scheme like that.

ROXANE.   The cadets will chew
    Their nails, but Cyrano will eat out his heart.
    And you'll have your revenge.

DE GUICHE (*coming closer*).   You love me, then –
    A little? When you make my enemies
    Your enemies – I'd like to see that as a sign
    Of love –

ROXANE (*backing away*).
              It could be – the sign of a start –

    DE GUICHE *takes documents from a satchel. He is, for the
    moment, businesslike.*

DE GUICHE. These are the orders for the companies,
    Signed, sealed, not yet delivered. This
    Is for the Guards. I'll keep it. Cyrano,
    So much for you, you battle-truffling swine.
    And so you too, Roxane, you like to play
    Your little games?

ROXANE (*watching him with some apprehension*).
                    Sometimes.
DE GUICHE.   Sometimes I say
   To myself that you and I are two of a kind.
   But always I'm mad about you. Now – to find
   Love trembling within you – when I have to go –
   Intolerable. Listen. Half a mile or so
   From here, in the rue d'Orléans, the order of
   Capuchins has its centre of brotherly love,
   Under Father Athanasius. Accordingly to
   Their rule, no layman may enter. But who
   Can bar the nephew of Richelieu? Their sleeves
   Are wide enough to hide me. The regiment leaves
   For the siege tonight, but without me. One
   More day will make no difference. Later on
   Tonight I'll come to you – masked.
ROXANE.   I apologize
   For mentioning the word – but – honour. Eyes,
   Spies will be watching. If anyone should
   Find out –
DE GUICHE. Pooh!
ROXANE.   The war, your duty, the good
   Of your family name –
DE GUICHE.   A lot of nonsense. I've
   A more urgent duty, a greater good – to contrive
   The voluntary surrender of – Say yes.
   Say it now.
ROXANE.   No.
DE GUICHE.   Say it. Whisper it.
ROXANE.   My
   Duty is to make you do yours. But –
DE GUICHE.   Bless
   You for that *but*.
ROXANE.   Oh no, you must go. Go. I

Must make myself make you go. I must order you
To be my hero.

DE GUICHE.   So you *can* love – can
Truly love –

ROXANE.   When I tremble for the safety of a man,
I may talk of love –

DE GUICHE.   And yet you say I must go?

ROXANE. Yes, in the name of love, my dear dear friend.

DE GUICHE. I go then. This adieu means not an end
But a beginning. Later, then. Later, Roxane.

He kisses his hand effusively at her, bows, leaves. The
DUENNA *comes on, making a mock reverence.*

DUENNA. My dear dear friend.

ROXANE.   Say nothing about
What I did just then. If Cyrano finds out
I stole his war from him –

DUENNA.   Yes, yes.

ROXANE (*calling*).   Cyrano!
(*To her* DUENNA)
I must keep up appearances. We must still go
To this discourse on the Tender Passion.

DUENNA.   All right,
But you've your own Tender Passion to attend to.

ROXANE.   I
know.
But Alcondre and Lysimon are speaking tonight.

DUENNA. And you're not going to listen.

CYRANO (*coming out*).   Listen, do.
Monkey-chatter can be instructive.

DUENNA (*going towards the other house*). See –
They've muffled the knocker, so that we
Shan't give the Tender Passion a heart attack.

ROXANE (*to Cyrano*).
When Christian comes to see me, tell him to wait.

CYRANO. Wait? But don't you make him dissertate
On a subject picked in advance?
DUENNA.   Monsieur Bergerac,
We're going in. Come on, madame, we're late.
ROXANE. A subject?
CYRANO.   Subject.
ROXANE.   But you'll be quiet?
CYRANO.   Dumb
As a wall, that's me.
ROXANE.   Nothing – no, everything.
Whatever singing fantasies shall come
Unbidden to his brain – on the subject of,
Naturally, love.
CYRANO.   Naturally. Love.
ROXANE. I'll tell him to overwhelm me with excess,
To rhapsodize, be brilliant.
CYRANO.   Good.
ROXANE (*fingers to lips*).   But – shhhh.
CYRANO (*fingers to lips*).
Shhhh, as you say.
ROXANE.   Not a word.
CYRANO.   Thanks very muchhhh.
ROXANE. Totally unprepared.
CYRANO.   Heavens, yes.
BOTH (*fingers to lips*).   Shhhh.

The DUENNA *having knocked, the door having been
opened, the two ladies go in.* CYRANO *goes to the edge of the
garden and calls.*

CYRANO. Christian!

CHRISTIAN *appears, very fashionably dressed now.*

                  Come and have the lines thrown to you.
I have your theme. All that you have to do,
You lucky, lucky, lucky, is to get

Your memory ready. This is your best chance yet
To cover yourself in genius. So let's go
Round to your lodgings. We don't have much time.
Come on, now, try to look intelligent.

CHRISTIAN (*forcefully*).   No!

CYRANO. No harm in trying to look intelli – Oh,
   You mean . . .?

CHRISTIAN.   That's right, my friend, I mean that I'm
   Going to stay here, going to wait for her.

CYRANO. But this is mad, this is the most head-reeling
   Vertiginous lunacy. Come on, come now, sir,
   Come and learn your lines.

CHRISTIAN.   No, I'm feeling
   Rebellious tonight. I'm tired, yes tired
   Of borrowing your lines, your letters, saying
   What you tell me to say, dithering with stage-fright.
   Oh, it was fine at first, it was like playing
   A sort of game. But now, at last, tonight,
   I'm past all fear. Tonight I feel inspired
   With my own inspiration. I no longer doubt
   That she loves me. My own words crash out.

CYRANO. Limp out, trickle out. Come on.

CHRISTIAN.   No. I'm not
   Entirely an analphabetic sot,
   As you'll see. Thanks to you, I've learned a lot.

CYRANO (*sardonically*).
   As I see.

CHRISTIAN. And, though I can't yet make
   The verbal summits, I know enough to take,
   \ By God, a woman in my arms.

CYRANO.   Bravo.

   ROXANE *and her* DUENNA *come out of the neighbouring
   house, along with exquisites of both sexes.* CYRANO *nods
   with grim satisfaction and starts to go. But* CHRISTIAN *loses
   his confidence.*

CHRISTIAN (*frightened*).
  It's her – it's she – don't leave me, Cyrano!
CYRANO. You're on your own, monsieur. Good luck.
    Goodnight.

  And so he marches off. CHRISTIAN *trembles.*

ROXANE (*to her friends*).
  Good night, Barthénoide, Grémione,
  Alcandre, Urimédonte –
DUENNA (*insincerely*).   I was quite
  Looking forward to that lecture.

    ROXANE *sees* CHRISTIAN *and calls him. The* DUENNA *nods*
    indulgently and goes into the house. The exquisites and
    précieuses leave the stage. The lovers are alone.

ROXANE.   Christian!
  Christian, you came. No matter that I missed
  That discourse by an amorous theorist
  Or theoretical amorist. Now the best
  Of all of them is here. The air is sweet.
  Evening is come. We are alone. That seat
  Beckons. Talk. I'll listen. Shall we sit?

    They seat themselves on that downstage bench. There is a
    silence, expectant on ROXANE's *part, wretched on* CHRIST-
    IAN's. *At length he breaks it.*

CHRISTIAN. I love you.
ROXANE.   So. Your theme. Embroider it,
  Weave gorgeous tapestries.
CHRISTIAN.   Love you.
ROXANE.   Rhapsodies.
CHRISTIAN. I love you so much.
ROXANE.   So much. Good. And
  Then?
CHRISTIAN. And then – I would – I would be glad if you

Loved me too. Say that you love me too.
ROXANE (*pouting*).
You offer skimmed milk when I ask for cream.
Tell me *how* you love me.
CHRISTIAN.   Very much.
ROXANE.   Turn your theme
Into a loving labyrinth. Devote
Your discourse to the true Platonic note.
CHRISTIAN (*growling*).
Oh God – I want to kiss your – kiss your throat.
ROXANE. Really!
CHRISTIAN.   I love you.
ROXANE.   That again?
CHRISTIAN.   Oh no,
I do not love you.
ROXANE.   Good.
CHRISTIAN.   I adore you.
ROXANE.   Oh,
This is too much.

   She gets up. CHRISTIAN *too has to rise.*

CHRISTIAN.   Forgive me, Roxane, I'm so
In love I'm growing stupid.
ROXANE.   I agree,
And that displeases me as much as though
You were growing ugly.
CHRISTIAN.   Listen –
ROXANE.   Retrieve
Your scattered eloquence. Otherwise – leave.
CHRISTIAN. But I –
ROXANE.   I know. You love me. Goodnight.
CHRISTIAN.   Stay!
Wait – listen – what I have to say
Is –
ROXANE.
     That you adore me. Good. Now go away.

She enters the house in a great huff. CHRISTIAN *is desperate.*
CYRANO *comes on.*

CYRANO. A great success. Felicitations.
CHRISTIAN.   For God's sake
   Help me.
CYRANO.   Ah no.
CHRISTIAN.   I shall die, here and now,
   If here and now I find no way to make
   Her love me again.
CYRANO.   Heavens, you idiot, how
   Do you expect me, here and now, to –

   A light goes on in Roxane's upper window. CHRISTIAN *is
   the first to see it.*

CHRISTIAN.   Wait –
   Look – see –
CYRANO (*touched*).
            Her window.
CHRISTIAN (*stentorianly*).
                        I shall die.
CYRANO. Not so much noise.
CHRISTIAN (*whispering*).   Die.
CYRANO (*looking up*).   Hm – a cloudy sky.
CHRISTIAN. Yes? Yes? Will you –?
CYRANO.   To reinstate
   You may not be easy. Still, we have to try.
   Stand there, in front of the balcony, while I
   Stand underneath and whisper the right words.
CHRISTIAN (*dubiously*).
   But –

   The PAGES *return.* CYRANO *addresses them.*

CYRANO. Welcome back, my unmelodious birds.

You've serenaded Montfleury? Good. Now,
You go to the corner of the street
And you go *there*. Wait for approaching feet.
If anyone comes by, play something –

They start off. He hales them back.

Wait.
A sad tune for a man – don't demonstrate –
And for a lady something shrill and sweet.
All right, all right, be off with you.

The PAGES *leave, severally.*

CHRISTIAN.   Now how
Do we start?
CYRANO.   Call her.
CHRISTIAN.   Roxane!
CYRANO.   A pebble or two.

*He throws some pebbles at the window, then he gets under
the balcony, while* CHRISTIAN *stands in front of it.* ROXANE
appears.

ROXANE. Was somebody calling?
CHRISTIAN.   Me. I.
ROXANE.   Who?
CHRISTIAN. Christian.
ROXANE (*disdainfully*). So.
CHRISTIAN.   I *have* to talk to you.
ROXANE. You've nothing to say to me.
CHRISTIAN.   Oh, please–*please*–
ROXANE. It's clear that you love me no longer.
CHRISTIAN (*to whom* CYRANO *whispers the right words*).
                                      Such heresies...
Such unjust slanders... Oh, you divinities...
Whose name is justice... witness that I love
More than mere words... can bear the burden of...

ROXANE. Better.

CHRISTIAN.   Love . . . that I had thought . . . a quiet
    child
    Discloses moods . . . so intemperate . . . and wild . . .
    He crushes my . . . cradling heart.

ROXANE.   Hm. Better still.
    But is it not best to break that unruly will
    And strangle such a monster?

CHRISTIAN.   Heavens, I've tried
    To commit that . . . venial infanticide,
    But . . . the tough atomy . . . I thought to seize . . .
    And crush . . . turned out an infant Hercules.

ROXANE. Good. Very good.

CHRISTIAN.   His first act was . . . to ride
    And rend . . . two hissing serpents . . . Doubt and Pride.

ROXANE. Quite excellent. But, since you mention doubt,
    Why do your words come so – haltingly out?
    It's as if your fancy suffered from, well –

CYRANO (*in an approximation to Christian's voice*).
                                Gout?

Roxane tinkles a laugh.

    Quick, this is getting difficult.

ROXANE.   Tonight
    You hesitate so strangely. Why?

CYRANO.   A good
    Question, and my answer is: each word
    Gropes through the darkness, looking for your light.

ROXANE. If that were really so, my own words would
    Limp, just like yours. Come, try a less absurd
    Explanation.

CYRANO.   Very well. Taste this:
    My heart is open wide – your words can't miss
    So large a target. Or, heavy with the honey of
    Desire, it zigzags to the orifice

Of your tiny ear, and buzzes blunderingly,
Seeking its way in, its wings a haze of love.
Or, should these not suffice, then, finally,
Since your words fall, they yield to gravity:
Mine have to rise and fight it.

ROXANE.   It seems to me
They fight less hard now than they had to do
A moment ago.

CYRANO.   Ah, but a moment or two
Of loosening up in the gymnasium
Works wonders.

ROXANE.   Am I so far above you still?

CYRANO. So far, I fear, that one hard word could kill,
Crushing my heart like a stone.

ROXANE.   Oh, then I'll come
Down to you.

CYRANO.   No!

ROXANE.   But I want to see you. Stand
On that bench there –

CYRANO.   No!

ROXANE.   Such a vehement *no*.
What *is* the matter?

CYRANO.   To hold in my hand
Such exquisite joy – I dare not let go
This precious chance to speak to you – unseen.

ROXANE. Unseen?

CYRANO.   A disembodied spirit, clean
Of the clogs of accident and decay. You see
A cloak of trailing blackness; you to me
Are a white gown of summer. I am a shadow
And you the quintessence of light. How can you know
What it means to roam this transitory meadow
Sunlit through the darkness? If ever – oh,
If ever I was eloquent –

ROXANE.   You were –

Very eloquent.

CYRANO.   But you have never heard till now
My true heart truly speaking.

ROXANE.   Why not?

CYRANO.   There
Was a certain obliquity, a sort of haze
Caused by this vertigo, this drunkenness
That afflicts all those who tremble in your presence.
But this one night it seems that I address
Your heart for the first time.

ROXANE.   The first time, yes.
Your very voice is changed.

CYRANO.   My heart's true essence
Is emboldened by this darkness to speak out.
It is myself that speaks. Where was I? Oh, forgive
This confusion, which is to me a heap
Of rose petals, a fantasy of sleep
So new, and so delicious.

ROXANE.   New?

CYRANO.   To live
A moment breathing your sustaining air,
Freed from the choking asthma of the fear
That you might laugh at me –

ROXANE.   Laugh at you? Why?

CYRANO. Because of the unworthiness of a fool,
An insufficiency that seeks to clothe
Itself in a sunset of words. How often I
Come to pluck Hesperus out of the sky
And end by plucking flowers because I loathe
A presumption that might spark your ridicule.

ROXANE. There's good in flowers, there's sweetness.

CYRANO.   Yes,
yes,
But not enough sweetness in all of the flowers of the
earth
For us, tonight.

ROXANE.   You have never spoken like this,
  Never before.
CYRANO.   Shatter them all, these tokens –
  Valentine hearts, arrows, the tinselled quiver,
  Stale words, stale honey sipped in finicking drops
  From tarnished gilded cups. What are they worth
  Compared to the wild urge that shouts, that beckons
  Our bodies to plunge and drown in the wild river?
ROXANE. But the soul, the spirit – ?
CYRANO.   You mean the petty
    rhymes
  Wrung from what petty spirits call the soul.
  I have made enough of those for you at times
  When I did not dare to bare myself, as now,
  To the overwhelming torrent of the night
  With its panic perfumes. Oh, my God, must we
  Insult nature by burbling nugacities   *rare*
  When those gold nuggets, myriad on myriad,
  Enflame the heavens? Our little alchemy,
  Distilling civilized exquisitries –
  Might it not, in its crass self-regard,
  Volatilize true feeling to the wind,
  And, dripping wordlets, miss the one true word?
ROXANE. Oh, but – poetry. You can't say that
  Of poetry –
CYRANO.   Poetry – rhyme – a game of words.
  Ah, love's too stark a force to tolerate
  Such tinklings, such tinkerings. A moment comes –
  And God help those for whom it never comes –
  When love of such nobility possesses
  This shaking frame that even the sweetest word,
  The ultimate honey, stings like vinegar –
ROXANE.   If so,
  What, when the moment comes for both of us,
  What words will you say?

CYRANO. In that most precious
Instant, I shall take all words that ever were,
Or weren't, or could, or couldn't be, and in
Mad armfuls, not bouquets, I'll smother you in them.
Oh God, how I love you, I choke with love, I
Stumble in madness, tread a fiery region
Where reason is consumed, I love you beyond
The limits that love sets himself, I love,
I love. Your name, Roxane, swings like a brazen
Bell, telling itself – Roxane, Roxane –
In my heart's belfry, and I tremble –
Roxane, Roxane – with each bronze, gold,
Silver reverberation. Listen, I swing
Down the rope to earth's level, to each small thing
– Trivial, forgettable, unforgettable by me –
That ever you do or did. A year ago,
The twelfth of May it was, at noon's striking,
You left your house with your hair dressed a different
    way,
The former way not being to your liking, ·
And you know how, when you've been looking at the
    sun,
You see red suns everywhere, embossed
On everything, so that solar flood of your hair
Blinded me and bequeathed an after-image
Of heavenly goldness touching everything
With a royal touch.
ROXANE (*shaken*). Yes – this is – love.
CYRANO. Love, the parasitic heavenly host,
A terribly jealous god has seized me with most
Wretched fury – and yet he seeks not to possess,
He is only mad to give. So my happiness
Is there to augment yours – even though
You forget, or never knew, the scourge of its flow.
I ask no more than to listen, twice, or thrice,

To the laughter born out of the sacrifice
Of mine. Each glance of your eyes begets some new
Virtue in me, new courage. Oh, can you
See this, feel it, understand? Do you sense
My heart rising towards you in this intense
Stillness, whose perfumed velvet wraps us close?
This night I speak, you listen. Never in my most
Reckless unreasonable dream have I hoped for this.
Now I can gladly die, knowing it is
My words that make you tremble in the blue
Shadow of the tree. For it is true –
You do tremble, like a leaf among the leaves,
Yes, and the passion of that trembling weaves
A spider filament that seeks me now,
Feeling its way along the jasmine bough.

ROXANE. Yes, I do tremble, and I weep, and I
    Am yours. I love, you have made me –

CYRANO.   Ah, to die,
    Death is all I need now after this
    Summit gained. I ask one thing –

CHRISTIAN (*bluntly breaking the spell*).
                         A kiss.

ROXANE. What?

CYRANO (*quietly seething*).
            Ooooooh.

ROXANE.   You asked for something.

CYRANO.   Yes –
    Too quick, too soon.

CHRISTIAN (*quietly but urgently*).
                Well, you got her into this
    State. Why shouldn't I get some benefit?

CYRANO. Yes, it's true. I did ask. But I was too
    Impetuous. I was – hurled into it.

ROXANE. You ask no more than that?

CYRANO.   No more?

CHRISTIAN (*eagerly*).   No. Yes.

CYRANO. No more is no more than a void, a nothingness.
   I asked too much, I ask you now to rebuff
   My importunity.

CHRISTIAN (*quietly shaking him*).
                   Why, why?

CYRANO.   Enough.
   Be quiet, Christian.

ROXANE.   What are you saying?

CYRANO.   Myself
   Was being angry with myself for going
   Too far. I said: 'Be quiet, Christian.'
   That was rude, I suppose. Somebody's coming –

   We hear from the distant PAGES *a bright tune and a sad
   accompaniment.*

By the sound of it, a woman *and* a man.

   An old CAPUCHIN *enters. He carries a lantern and is
   evidently looking for a particular address.* CYRANO *addresses him.*

Ah, I see what they mean – a priest. Diogenes?
   Back from the dead, looking for honesty?

CAPUCHIN. No, sir. The name is – er – Madame Robin.

CHRISTIAN. Here's a damned nuisance.

CYRANO.   You seem to be
   On the wrong track. Go straight.

   He points. The CAPUCHIN *nods his thanks.*

CAPUCHIN.   Thank you, my friend.
   I'll pray for you.

CYRANO.   May grace and fortune attend
   Your holy cucullus.

CAPUCHIN (*pausing, suspicious*).
                   Eh?

CYRANO.   Cucullus.

The CAPUCHIN *realizes, having forgotten the term, that*
CYRANO *means his hood. Satisfied, he moves on and off.*

CAPUCHIN.   Yes, yes, I see.
CHRISTIAN. Get that kiss for me.
CYRANO.   No.
CHRISTIAN.   That kiss for me.
CYRANO. No.
CHRISTIAN.   Sooner or later I –
CYRANO.   Sooner or later, true,
   It has to be, that labial conjunction,
   A historical necessity, since she
   Is beautiful and, all unworthy, you
   Glow in the perfume of the unearned unction
   Made up of youth and strength and comeliness.
   But I must be the agent of her *yes.*

      CHRISTIAN *grinds his teeth.* ROXANE, *who went in on the*
      appearance of the CAPUCHIN, *is out again on the balcony.*

ROXANE. Has he gone? Are you there?
CYRANO.   Yes.
ROXANE.   We were
      speaking of –
   Of a –
CYRANO. Kiss. The word is sweet enough,
   And yet your lips are shy of saying it.
   If the word burns them, what is your presage of
   The thing itself? Fear should consume you. Yet
   After all you've glided insensibly
   From mockery to a smile, from a smile to a sigh,
   From a sigh to a tear. Now slide from a tear to a kiss.
   It's but a heartbeat's distance from that to this.
ROXANE (*as ready, or almost, as* CHRISTIAN).
   Oh, do be quiet.
CYRANO (*comfortably settled for a lecture*).

          Soon. In a moment. How
Shall we define a kiss? The sacrament of a vow,
The lightly stamped seal of a promise, the endorsement
   of
A promissory note on the bank of love,
The very O of love in the expectant lips,
Eternity in the instant the bee sips,
The music of the spheres on the lark's wing,
A flower-tasting eucharist, a ring
Forged of two rings, red alchemized to gold.

ROXANE. Enough.

    CHRISTIAN *nods vigorously.*

CYRANO (*taking his time*).
          So noble a thing, that, so we're told,
The Queen of France could not, from her fabulous
   hoard,
Find a richer jewel to bestow on an English lord.

ROXANE (*impatiently*).
Indeed?

CYRANO. Indeed. And, like Lord Buckingham, I
Too have had my mournful silences, my
Unspeakable adoration of majesty – in you.
Like him, I am sad and faithful.

ROXANE.   Like him too
You are beautiful.

CYRANO.   So I am. I'd forgotten.

ROXANE.   Come.

CYRANO (*to* CHRISTIAN).
You heard what she said.

ROXANE.   Taste your flower.

    CHRISTIAN, *as before, is hesitant when it comes to the act.*

CYRANO. Get up there.

ROXANE.   Let us savour our

Souls conjoined in our lips.
CYRANO.　　　　　　　　　　　Now what
In hell's name are you waiting for?
CHRISTIAN.　　　　　　　　　　　　I'm not
Sure, really, this is the right time –
ROXANE.　　　　　　　　　　　Here's
Your instant infinity, your music of the spheres.
CYRANO. Mount, you animal!

He pushes CHRISTIAN *to the tree, whose branches he climbs
with ease to reach the balcony.* CHRISTIAN *takes* ROXANE *in
his arms. They kiss.*

CHRISTIAN.　　　　　　　　　　Ah – Roxane!
CYRANO (*not looking*).　　　　　　　　It appears
He's at his banquet – the banquet I prepared,
Only to end as its Lazarus. Still, I'm spared
One crumb, I suppose, one wishbone. And this is
The knowledge that it's my words that she kisses
And not his lips. So – let's be cheerful, then.

The double music starts up once more from the PAGES.

Woman? Man? It's that Capuchin again.

*He lightly runs into the shadows and then reappears,
running, as if just arriving.*

Ho, there!

ROXANE *and* CHRISTIAN *disengage.*

ROXANE.　　Who is it?
CYRANO.　　　　　　　Cyrano. Is Christian
Up there by any chance?
CHRISTIAN (*with a show of surprise*).
　　　　　　　　　　　Cyrano!
CYRANO.　　　　　　　　　That Capuchin
Is here again. It's something for you, Roxane.

You'd best come down.

> ROXANE *and* CHRISTIAN *go in. The* CAPUCHIN *appears.*

CAPUCHIN.   Madame Robin lives here. ·
I have it on very good authority.
CYRANO.   Rolin?
CAPUCHIN. Robin.
CYRANO.   I thought you said Rolin.
CAPUCHIN.   *Robin.*
  (*Bleating like a sheep*)
Robiiiiiiiin.
CYRANO.   I hear. It wasn't very clear
Before. One letter can make a difference. Not L – B.
CAPUCHIN (*suspiciously*).
  How did you know I have a letter? Oh, I see.
I see.

> ROXANE *and* CHRISTIAN *come out of the door.*

ROXANE. Letter?
CAPUCHIN.   For Madame Robin.
ROXANE.   I am she.
CAPUCHIN. A very noble lord gave it to me
To give to you.
ROXANE.   De Guiche!
CHRISTIAN.   He dares?
ROXANE.   He won't ·
Dare any more – not now.

> *They look at each other ardently and can hardly restrain themselves from embracing.*

CAPUCHIN.   Some holy matter, I don't
Doubt.

> ROXANE, *having torn open the letter, reads it to* CHRISTIAN *while* CYRANO *tries to interest the* CAPUCHIN *in horticulture.*

ROXANE. 'The drums are beating. The regiment
Is ready for the march. I have already sent
The story about that I have gone on ahead,
But in fact I'm here in the convent – as I said
I would be. I'm sending this by an old
Sheep–headed monk who, naturally, has not been told
Its content. I must see you tonight. I must.
Your smile both beckons and maddens. I hope and trust
You have already forgiven my audacity
And will give a welcome to him who hopefully
Sincerely etcetera etcetera.'
(*She addresses the* CAPUCHIN.)
                                        Father! This letter
Concerns you.
CAPUCHIN.   Does it? Does it?
ROXANE.   So I'd better
Read it to you.
CAPUCHIN.   Very well, very well.
ROXANE. It's terrible.
CAPUCHIN.   Come, my child.
ROXANE.   'Mademoiselle,
It seems His Eminence the Cardinal
Will have his way, whatever you say or do.
That is why I send this note to you
By a very holy, intelligent, discreet
Capuchin. Instruct him, please, to meet
These my instructions, which are that he is
At once, in your house, to perform the ceremonies
Of holy matrimony –' Oh, this is tyrannical.
CAPUCHIN. Courage, daughter.
ROXANE.   'His Grace the Cardinal
Demands the nuptials of you and Christian.
This is hard news, I know. But all that you can
Do is resign yourself to the command
Of His Eminence, who sends his blessing and

His wishes for much happiness. I end
With my own good wishes. Your humble friend,
Etcetera etcetera.'
CAPUCHIN.   I knew it, I knew
He was truly noble, one who could not do
A thing that was not wholly holy. Who
Is the bridegroom?

He looks at the two men. ROXANE *breaks down, or pretends
to.*

ROXANE.   Oh, this is awful.
CAPUCHIN (*to* CYRANO).   You?
The will of God, daughter, is often obscure.
CHRISTIAN. It's me – I am the bridegroom.
CAPUCHIN.   Are you sure?
ROXANE (*quickly*).
'Postscript. Give to the convent, in my name,
One hundred and twenty louis. Signed: the same.'
CAPUCHIN. A worthy lord. It's very rare to find
Blue blood allied to such a generous mind.
Daughter, resign yourself.
ROXANE.   I *am* resigned.
(*To* CYRANO)
De Guiche will come. For God's sake hold him there.
He mustn't enter before –
CYRANO (*to the* CAPUCHIN).   How long will it take?
CAPUCHIN. Oh, fifteen minutes, sir.
CYRANO.   You'd better make
It five. In. In. I need fresh air.

The CAPUCHIN *goes in with the soon-to-be-happy couple.*

I also need to distract his lordship. Where?
How? Up here. I think I have my plan.

*He gets up into the branches of the tree. Gloomy music
sounds.*

Ah, by the sound of it, a man,
Very much a man in a minor key.
Come, then. Not too high. Protect me, tree.

> DE GUICHE *fumbles his way on, masked.*

A matter of a voice? Will he know it's me?
Let me open the door to my origins. Cric crac.

> *He winds himself up like a toy. He speaks like a Gascon,
> not a Parisian. He puts his hat back to front and puts his
> cloak over it.*

Cyrano – be true de Bergerac.

DE GUICHE. Did that blasted Capuchin deliver? Damn this
    mask –
I can't see –

> CYRANO *leaps down gracefully.* DE GUICHE *starts.*

                    Where did you fall from, may I ask?
CYRANO. The moon.
DE GUICHE.   *The moon?*
CYRANO.   What time is it?
DE GUICHE.   Is he mad?
CYRANO. What time – country – day of the month – of the
    year?
DE GUICHE. Let me –

> *He tries to get to Roxane's front door.* CYRANO *stays in the
> way.*

CYRANO. I'm dizzy, dazed, befuddled –
DE GUICHE.   Monsieur –
CYRANO. I fell. I've fallen. You wish to know where from?
DE GUICHE. The moon, you said.
CYRANO.   The moon. Dropped like
    a bomb,
And I don't mean that metaphorically.

DE GUICHE (*trying to get past him*).
   Please –
CYRANO.   A second – maybe a century –
   I lost all sense of time during my fall.
   I was in this kind of saffron-coloured ball –
DE GUICHE.   Good. Let me pass.
CYRANO.   Where? Where? Don't
      trifle with
   This shattered sensorium. What is this place
   On which I've tumbled like an aerolith?
DE GUICHE.   An aerolith?
   Allow me –
CYRANO.   I had no choice, hurtling through space,
   Oh my point of arrival. *Where am I?* Ah, that face –
   Black – are you an oppressed colonial?
DE GUICHE.   This is a mask.
CYRANO.   Venice! A carnival!
DE GUICHE (*still trying to pass*).
   A lady is waiting for me.
CYRANO.   Ah, now I know –
   Paris. Where else could it be? Paris. So
   This is where the ethereal typhoon
   Has dumped me. What a voyage. Dust of the moon,
   Asteroid fragments cling like sleep to my eyes,
   Planet-fur on my spurs, blond comet-hairs
   On my coat –
DE GUICHE.   Allow me –
CYRANO.   Can you see the Great Bear's
   Toothmark in my calf? This bump on my thigh's
   From the hurled waterpot of Aquarius.
   You've no idea of the zodiacal fuss
   I initiated. I fell into one of the dishes
   Of Libra's scales, and look – scales from the Fishes
   – Hard to scrape off. Grab my nose with your fingers,
   Give it a squeeze and it will spurt out pure
   Milk –

DE GUICHE. *Please.*

CYRANO.   From the Milky Way. I broke a string as
   I glissaded over the Lyre. Ah, you can be sure
   There's a book in this, a perilous record of risks.
   I shall use these stars on my cloak as asterisks.

DE GUICHE. Good. Now if you'll excuse me —

CYRANO.   Do forgive.
   You're impatient to be apprised of the creatures that live
   In the lunar caverns, and to know the morphology
   Of its cucurbitous rotundity —

DE GUICHE. What I want now —

CYRANO.   Is to know how I got up
   There — My special invention, yes?

DE GUICHE.   Mad.

CYRANO.   First, I swear
   It has nothing to do with Regiomontanus's
   Eagle or Archytas's pigeon — ornithology
   Doesn't come into it — stupid birds, anyway.

DE GUICHE. Mad, but he's been to a university.

CYRANO. No! My mode of spatial travel is
   Painfully original. Mode — did I say?
   Modes. I've invented six techniques whereby
   To violate that blue virginity
   Up there.

   DE GUICHE *grows interested in spite of himself.*

DE GUICHE.   Six?

CYRANO.   Six. Let me specify.
   I strip myself as nude as a candle, place
   Around that nudity a carapace
   Covered with crystal vials of morning dew.
   The sun sucks up the dew, and sucks me too.

DE GUICHE. So. That's *one.*

CYRANO.   Another one. I escape
   From earth in a ship of icosahedral shape —

Stuck with ten burning mirrors. They rarefy
The air. The rare air lifts me, and I fly.

DE GUICHE. Two.

CYRANO. Or I mount a machine forged in the
figure
Of a grasshopper, activated by a trigger
That sets off successive charges of saltpetre.
I jerk off into space. What could be neater?
Sweeter?

DE GUICHE. Three.

CYRANO. Smoke always tends to soar.
I fill a globe with smoke and —

DE GUICHE. That makes four.

CYRANO. This next may seem fantastic. Bright Apollo,
Who rules the sun, he likes to suck and swallow
The marrow of the oxen of the sun.
I smear myself with that — and, swish, it's done.

DE GUICHE. Five.

CYRANO. Finally, monsieur, I sit or stand
Upon an iron plate. And in my hand
I clutch a magnet. This I throw — and — throw —
The iron lurches after, as you know.
I can do that indefinitely.

DE GUICHE. Six.
Which did you choose of these ingenious tricks
To make your recent voyage into heaven?
Not that I believe you.

CYRANO. Number seven.

DE GUICHE. And what's the seventh way?

CYRANO. You're going to
see.

CYRANO *makes strange noises and gestures*.

DE GUICHE. What?

CYRANO. Can't you guess what's happening to me?

DE GUICHE. No.

CYRANO.   It's nearly time, sir, for high tide.
The moon is calling.

*And, indeed, the moon, long occluded, has at last emerged
from behind the clouds.*

                              I must stand beside
The ocean, having wallowed in it first.
My hair is dripping wet. The lunar thirst
Pulls at it, then the rest of me. I soar
Free as an angel, as I did before,
Tumbling to earth a quarter of an hour ago.
The time, my lord, is up. And so –

DE GUICHE.   And so?

*CYRANO resumes his normal voice, adjusts his cloak and
hat. His nose shines in the moonlight.*

CYRANO. A marriage has been celebrated.

DE GUICHE.   What?
Am I drunk or something? That voice. It's not –
That nose – It is.

CYRANO (*with a courtly reverence*).
                    At your service. Cyrano.

The wedding procession appears, RAGUENEAU *and Roxane's* DUENNA *holding candles, the* DUENNA *crying, the two*
PAGES *– who must have entered the house by the back door –
playing festive music.* ROXANE *and* CHRISTIAN *beam.*

DE GUICHE. You! He! Clever, mademoiselle.

ROXANE. Baroness.

DE GUICHE (*to* CYRANO).
                    You, monsieur, you did that well.
You could have charmed a saint poised on the sill
Of heaven. You ought to write that book.

CYRANO.   I will.

CAPUCHIN. My lord, the knot is tied you bade me tie.
DE GUICHE. As I can see. You, *baroness*, bid goodbye
To your paint-fresh husband.
ROXANE.   Bid good– Why?
DE GUICHE (*to* CHRISTIAN).
    Your regiment leaves tonight, sir. Be so good
    As to report at once.
ROXANE.   You mean – for the war?
DE GUICHE. That is what regiments usually leave for,
    Milady.
ROXANE. But you – surely – I understood
The cadets were not going.
DE GUICHE.   They are and always were.
    (*To* CHRISTIAN)
Here is the order. Pray deliver it, sir.
ROXANE (*falling into her husband's arms*).
    Oh, Christian!
DE GUICHE (*sneering, to* CYRANO).
                         The wedding night is still a good
    Way off.
CYRANO.   That thought disturbs me less than it should.
CHRISTIAN. Your lips again –
CYRANO.   Come on. Enough. Let's go.
CHRISTIAN. Oh, you don't know how hard it is.
CYRANO.   I know.

    *Drums can be heard in the distance, also the shrilling of a
    trumpet.*

DE GUICHE. We're marching.

    He salutes sardonically and marches off.

ROXANE (*in great distress*).
                         Take care of him, Cyrano.
    Keep him out of danger.

CYRANO (*hanging on to* CHRISTIAN).
                              All right, I'll try,
But I can't really promise.
ROXANE.   Be sure he keeps warm and
    dry.
CYRANO. As far as is soldierly possible.
ROXANE.   Keep him away
From other women.
CYRANO.   Not even the odd little chat?
ROXANE. No! And make him write to me every day.
CYRANO (*at attention, emphatically*).
    Madame, I can certainly promise you that.

   √ *They go. The women weep.* RAGUENEAU *and the* PAGES
   wave. Drums and trumpets.

CURTAIN

Act IV

The Siege of Arras

We are at the post occupied by Captain Carbon de Castel-Jaloux's company. In the background there is a rampart; beyond it a plain stretches away to the horizon, with earthworks covering it. In the distance are the walls of Arras and the silhouette of its roofs against the sky. There are tents, weapons, drums, a campfire. SENTRIES *stand at spaced-out intervals. Some of the* CADETS *sleep round the fire, under blankets. It is a cold dawn.* LE BRET *and* CARBON *keep watch: they are pale and emaciated.* CHRISTIAN, *asleep, is even more so; he is also restless. There is as yet no sign of Cyrano.*

LE BRET. Shocking.
CARBON.   Very.
LE BRET.   Intolerable.
CARBON.   Intolerably so.
LE BRET (*loudly*).
  God curse it!
CARBON.   If *you* want to curse, keep it low.
  You'll wake them.

    Some of the sleepers stir.

                        Shhhh. Sleep, sleep.
  Who sleeps, dines.

LE BRET.   Who takes a nap takes a snack.
  But if, like me, you're an insomniac
  You don't get much in the way of dinners, you know.

  There is firing offstage. LE BRET *is angry.*

God damn that blasted insomniac musketry.
It'll wake our babies.

  Men raise their heads from their blankets.

                          Sleep, deep, deep.
  It isn't reveille yet.

  There is more firing.

CARBON.   Just the usual crack
  At Cyrano coming back home.

  The raised heads are lowered.

A SENTRY (*offstage*).   Halt, who goes there?
CYRANO (*offstage*).
  Cyrano de Bergerac.
ANOTHER SENTRY (*on the parapet*).
                          Halt, who –
CYRANO (*appearing*).

                          Bergerac,
  Imbecile.
LE BRET.   Thank God, as usual, you're back.
CYRANO (*descending, motioning him not to waken the sleepers*).
  Shhhhh.
CARBON.   Not wounded yet?
CYRANO.   No, they've got
  Into the habit of missing me.
LE BRET.   Risking your life
  Before breakfast to post a letter – mad. Not,
  Of course, that there *is* any breakfast.
CYRANO.   What

Must be done must be done. I promised his wife,
As I must call her, that he'd speak to her by post
If he couldn't speak on the pillow. Pale as a ghost,
Poor devil, starving to death.

CARBON.   We all are.

CYRANO.   I know,
But he seems to show it more than most.
If only that poor child could see him – Still handsome,
    though.

LE BRET.   You'd better get some sleep.

CYRANO.   Don't growl at me,
You old mother-bear, and don't worry either. I'm
Pretty careful crossing the Spanish lines.
I just wait till they're drunk.

CARBON.   You might
Consider bringing something back sometime
For us.

LE BRET.   *Jamòn. Huevos. Vino.*

CYRANO.   I would if I
Didn't, as you know, have to travel light.
Today, though, there appear to be signs
That the French are going to dine or else to die.

CARBON.   What signs?

CYRANO.   I'm not sure. But you'll see.

LE BRET.   What a
    mess.
We're besieging Arras, and yet it's we
Who are doing the starving.

CARBON.   Besieging Arras, yes.
And all the while His Eminent Gorgeousness
The Cardinal Prince of Spain is besieging *us*.

CYRANO.   Perhaps somebody will get down to besieging
    him.

LE BRET.   Not funny. Our chances don't get any better,
And yet you grin instead of looking grim.

Risking your life every day to send a letter.
You're unnatural. What sort of a father and mother –
Never mind. Where are you going?
CYRANO.   To write another.

*He goes into a tent. Drums signal the dawn. We hear the
distant voices of officers waking their men.*

CARBON. Damned drums. Another nutritious sleep
Gone to the devil. Poor devils. I know
What their first words are going to be.

The CADETS *wake, groaning.*

FIRST CADET.   God, I'm so
Hungry.
CARBON (*prodding the sleepers*).
            Come on, out of it.
SECOND CADET.   Oh, no.
THIRD CADET. Not one step.
FOURTH CADET (*looking in a polished cuirasse*).
                               Yellow as saffron cake,
My tongue.
FIFTH CADET (*waking with a start*).
            Cake – who said cake?
FIRST CADET.   Very indigestible air,
This time of day.
CARBON.   Come on.
SECOND CADET.   I'm not going to make
Another move.
THIRD CADET.   I'd give my coronet
For a mousetrap. And I wouldn't care
Whether it was cheese or mouse that I found there.
SIXTH CADET (*looking out of his tent*).
I tell you this: if my stomach doesn't get
Something to stop its roaring, it's going to stay,
Like Achilles, in its tent all day.

LE BRET (*at Cyrano's tent-flap*).

Cyrano – come out.

FOURTH CADET.   Bread before bullets.

I'm perfectly prepared to forgo the butter.

LE BRET (*more urgently*).

Cyrano – come on. There's a mutinous mutter

Ready to brew. Take their minds off their gullets.

Tell them a tale or something –

THIRD CADET (*rushing up to* FIRST CADET).

                              What's that you're chewing?

FIRST CADET. Gun wad fried in the choicest axle grease.

Good rich country, this. Would you care for a piece?

> *Two* CADETS *enter, one with a gun, the other with a fishing rod.*

SEVENTH CADET. Home from the hunt.

EIGHTH CADET.   Fishing in the river

Scarpe.

> *The other* CADETS *rush to them. They yell severally.*

CADETS. What have you got there? Fish? Game? Pheasant? Carp?

EIGHTH CADET. A gudgeon.

SEVENTH CADET.   A sparrow.

CADETS.   Mutiny!

LE BRET (*with great urgency*).   Cyrano!

> CYRANO *comes tranquilly from his tent, a pen in one hand, a book in the other, a helmet on his head.*

CYRANO. This noise is very distracting.

> *There is a guilty silence.* CYRANO *addresses* FIRST CADET.

                              You. I see

You've something on your mind.

FIRST CADET.   My stomach.

CYRANO.   We
   All suffer the same vacuity.
SECOND CADET. But you seem to enjoy it.
CYRANO.   Good for the
   figure.
THIRD CADET. Something to eat, for God's sake.
CYRANO.   There are
   bigger
   Things than food. Still – one salad bowl.

> *He takes off his helmet and places it on the ground. The*
> CADETS *look into it as though, by magical conjuration, food*
> *will appear in it.*

SECOND CADET. I don't see any salad.
CYRANO.   Feed your soul
   With Homer's *Iliad.*

> *He throws in the book. The* CADETS *growl.*

FIRST CADET.   Oh God, when I
   Think of all those swine guzzling away
   Back in Paris at their six meals a day,
   Like his Holy Grace and Cardinal – grrrr –
CYRANO (*reasonably*).   But
   Why envy His Grace his grease? Better to die
   Of inanition than a loaded gut.
   The gate of heaven is narrow, and the thin
   Man has the easier chance of sidling in.
FIRST CADET (*angrily*).
   Don't try to feed us with epigrams. Fine words
   Butter no parsnips.
SECOND CADET (*deliriously*).
                   Parsnips – in a white sauce.
THIRD CADET. I don't much care for parsnips. Oh, good
   Lord, what am I saying?
CYRANO.   *I* am saying this:

I'd rather die on pointed elegances –
Fine words, as you call them – under a sky
Of saffron sunset than wail and weep and cry
About my rumbling innards. Rather die
Saying a good thing for a good cause
Than dream of licking goose-grease from my paws,
Die at the hands of a worthy enemy
Rather than be degraded by the eclipse
Of death in a soft bed. I want to depart
This life with honourable steel piercing my heart
And a piercing epigram upon my lips.
SECOND CADET. But we're hungry.
CYRANO.   The whole world's
    hungry. You
Think only of yourselves.

> *We now notice that the old* FLUTEPLAYER *of the company has come in starving but stoical. He sits at the back of the stage.* CYRANO *addresses him.*

                              Here, Bertrandou –
Old shepherd as you were, play on your pipe
To these poor little lambs who grouse and gripe
At the griping of their guts. Put pipe to mouth
And pipe some of the old airs of the south,
Whose every note smiles like a little sister,
In which we hear, through a nostalgic mist, a
Smoke of memory, the voices of friends –
A melody whose lazy line ascends
Like the thin woodsmoke of the cottages
Of our homeland – a pungent tune that is
The very distillation of our speech.
Your flute, that gnarled old warrior, let him reach
Back, while your fingers touch the stops and dance
A minuet of sparrows, beyond the chance
That chose him, shaped him, notched him, changed him to

A little glory of ebony. Let him, through you,
Recall his days as a reed of the river, before
He lost his innocence and went to war.

    BERTRANDOU *plays a melancholy folk tune.*

Listen, you Gascons, now you hear no more
The shrilling martial fife. It's a woodland cry,
Not a banshee of the battle shrieking high
But the cool cantilene the goatherds finger.
Listen – it's the hill where the night mists linger,
The valley, and the good earth like red meat,
The plains like a storm of emeralds, the sweet
Greenness of spring nights on the Dordogne.
Listen, you Gascons – it is all Gascogne.

    *They listen quietly to the flute tune. The odd tear is
    furtively wiped.*

CARBON. You're making them cry.
CYRANO.   Yes – out of
    homesickness,
A nobler hunger than that of the flesh.
They're feeling a starvation in their hearts,
Not in their viscera.
CARBON.   Still, it hurts
    Their manhood.
CYRANO.   Weakens them? Not so. I'll flush
    The heroic scarlet to their arteries
    Back in an instant. All that's needed is –

    *He makes a signal. The drums start beating. The CADETS
    start up, rush for their arms, run to the parapet.*

CADETS. What – where – what is it – where is it?
CYRANO (*to* CARBON).   See?

    *But the CADETS think that CYRANO was warning them of
    the approach of their colonel. He is coming.*

SECOND CADET. Ach – Monsieur de Guiche is on his way.
THIRD CADET. He makes me –
FOURTH CADET.   Not so much as he makes
me.

They return to their former positions, depressed.

FOURTH CADET. Sick, eh? You're not the only ones.
What with the lace collar on his corselet –
THIRD CADET. Always the little courtier –
FOURTH CADET.   Very much
The nephew of the cardinal.
CYRANO (*always fair*).   Nevertheless,
Gentlemen, he's one of Gascony's sons.
THIRD CADET. A counterfeit. The real Gascons, us,
Are a bit mad, but he's a bit too sane.
Rational. A rational Gascon's dangerous.
LE BRET. He's pale. At least he shows that common touch.
FOURTH CADET. Oh, nobody doubts that he can feel the
pain.
Of hunger, just like us poor bastards, but
Those jewels on his belt make the cramps in his gut
Sort of glitter, like the sun on ice.
CYRANO. Do you want him to see you suffering? Get out
your dice,
Your cards. Smoke your pipes. Come on there, try and
look
As if you liked this famine. I'll read this book –
Descartes.

The CADETS *obey.* CYRANO, *who has taken the volume
from his pocket, starts to read. Silence.* DE GUICHE *comes
in, elegant but haggard.*

DE GUICHE. Good morning.

There is a silence.

Black looks as usual, eh? Right, gentlemen –
The mountain-hovel nobility, the beefless barons
A la sauce béarnaise, the Périgord princelings are
Above respecting their colonel. Very well, then.
Knowing the squalor of your rabbit warrens,
I know how little your code of conduct matters.
Call me a crawling courtier, a politician,
Resent my steel covered with Genoese lace.
I spurn your standards. To be a proper patrician
You have to be a pauper. It's a foul disgrace
To be a Gascon and not go in tatters.
This dumb insolence asks for punishment. I've a mind
To leave that task to your captain. You, sir, find
Something fitting in the *Manual
of Military Law*.

CARBON.   I'm afraid that's impossible.
I pay my men from my own pocket. And I obey
Battle orders only.

DE GUICHE.   Indeed? Well, you and they
Will soon have your chance of obedience. I see
Your prospective resentment. Jealousy!
Your conduct under fire, apparently,
Doesn't compare with mine in any way.
How many of you, squatting on your haunches,
Could do the thing that I did yesterday?
I lashed the Count de Bucquoi out of Bapaume,
Pouring my men on his in avalanches.
I charged three times.

CYRANO (*without looking up from his book*).
                          But you failed to bring home
Your white scarf.

DE GUICHE (*pleased*). So it's already got around,
That story, has it?

CYRANO.   Tell us.

DE GUICHE.   When

The third charge beckoned and I was rallying my men,
To my astonishment I suddenly found
I was being thrust with a throng of fugitives
Into the enemy's lines. The Spaniard gives
No quarter – I was in danger of being shot.
So what did I do? Thought quickly. Got
Shot of the white scarf that marks my rank
And thus – anonymous, inconspicuous, blank –
Escaped and rallied my own force. Ah yes,
It worked. From the brink of death to a crash
Of victory. What do you think, my friend,
Of that little display of resourcefulness?
CYRANO. This. A man's white plume is his panache,
His visible soul, not a thing to lend or spend.
It's the shining badge of his scorn of his enemies.
Henry of Navarre, Henry the Fourth of France,
Outnumbered in the enemy's advance,
Never even dreamed of jettisoning his.

Quiet satisfaction is registered among the CADETS.

DE GUICHE. But the point is: my device was a success.
CYRANO. True. But an officer never resigns easily
His privilege of being a target for the enemy.
Your courage and mine differ in this, monsieur –
If I'd been present at that heroic affair,
When you dropped your scarf I'd have picked it up then
and there
And worn it myself.
DE GUICHE. Always boasting.
CYRANO. No.
Lend it to me tonight and I'll lead the charge
With your white scarf over my shoulder.
DE GUICHE. Ah, these large
And vacuous gasconnades. You're safe, as you know,
With that offer. Our intelligence understands

That that sector still lies in the enemy's hands,
And my scarf lies on the river bank. The river
Is swept by their artillery. No one could ever
Reach that scarf alive.

*CYRANO slowly draws the scarf from his pocket. He hands it
to DE GUICHE without moving from his place. Indeed, he
turns a page of his Descartes. The quiet satisfaction of the
CADETS is manifested in jubilant pipe-puffs. DE GUICHE
shows no emotion. He takes the scarf.*

CYRANO.   With my compliments.
DE GUICHE. Thank you. This bit of white will do very well
  To make a signal – a signal, that, to tell
  The truth, I was hesitant about making.
  But now, gentlemen, no more hesitance.

He gets up on to the parapet and waves the scarf vigorously.

SENTRY. Look – there's a man there running away.
DE GUICHE.   And
    taking
  My signal with him. My pet Spanish spy.

*The CADETS no longer now affect indifference. CYRANO is
alert.*

CYRANO. Spy?
DE GUICHE.   Yes. He tells his masters what I
  Pay him to tell them.
CYRANO (*with disgust*).   A traitor.
                              I suppose so,
DE GUICHE.
  But a very useful traitor. Now, what was it we
  Were talking about? Ah yes. You may as well know
  Our marshal's plan. You might find it interesting.
  Last night we saw an opportunity,
  With reasonable luck, of revictualling

The army. In silence, covered by a good black
Night, the marshal marched to Doulens, where
Our supplies are. There's a very fair chance that he
Will reach them. But to be sure of getting back
In safety, he's taken an exceptionally
Large force with him. A good half of our army
Is absent from the camp.

CYRANO.   Thank God the enemy
   Don't know that.

DE GUICHE (*smiling*).
                       Oh, but they do, they do.
   They're going to attack us.

CYRANO.   Ah.

CARBON.   Ah.

DE GUICHE.   My spy,
   A very reliable and pliable spy who
   Tells me everything, asked me where I would
   Prefer the Spanish attack to be made. My reply
   Was that he should go out and wait between
   The lines and watch for my signal. That point should
   Be the point of the Spanish advance.

CARBON.   You mean –?

DE GUICHE (*expansively*).
   I mean, gentlemen, that this is all for you.

CARBON. Very well, let's get ready.

DE GUICHE.   Another hour.

FIRST CADET (*sardonically*).   Oh,
      good.

DE GUICHE. As you will doubtless all have understood,
   The aim is to gain time. We're not sure when
   The marshal will return.

CARBON.   And to gain this time?

DE GUICHE (*blandly*).
   Gentlemen, you will all be so very good
   As to lay down your lives.

CYRANO (*with equal blandness*).
                              Would it be reasonable
  To call this – well, revenge?
DE GUICHE.   I won't pretend
  That I care the least damn about any of you.
  But since you all consider you're no end
  Of fine brave warriors and – this is hard to do,
  Admittedly – leaving out the personal,
  You're the obvious choice. If you want that to mean
  I serve my king by serving my own spleen,
  I will not contradict you.
CYRANO (*pleasantly*).   Well, that's candid.
  May we offer our thanks?
DE GUICHE (*sneering*).   You, sir, whose bliss
  Is to engage a hundred singlehanded,
  Ought to be rather looking forward to this.

    CYRANO *turns his back on him and addresses the* CADETS.

CYRANO. There are, as you know, six chevrons on the old
  Arms of Gascony, six – blue and gold.
  There's going to be a seventh. You don't need me
  To tell you what the colour has to be.

    All this time CHRISTIAN *has been seated quietly, unmoved,
    unhearing, arms resignedly crossed.* CYRANO *goes over to
    him.*

  Christian –
CHRISTIAN (*quietly*).
              Roxane.
CYRANO.   I know.
CHRISTIAN. I should like to say goodbye to her, to put
  My whole heart –
CYRANO.   In a letter. I thought of that.
CHRISTIAN. Let me see it.
CYRANO.   You really want to?

CHRISTIAN.   Why not?
  I'm supposed to have written it.

    CYRANO *somewhat reluctantly takes a package from his*
    breast and hands it to CHRISTIAN. CHRISTIAN *looks curious-*
    ly at something on it.

                           What?

CYRANO. Yes?
CHRISTIAN.   This spot – this little circle – to me
  It looks very much like a tear.
CYRANO (*embarrassed*).   Oh, well, you know
  How it is. When a poet writes a poem, he
  Is frequently moved by his own fiction. I admit
  I've written a moving letter. I tried
  Not to be moved, but I *was* moved. Just a bit.
CHRISTIAN (*wonderingly*).
  You mean to say – you *cried*?
CYRANO (*stoutly*).   Yes. I cried.
  And why not? Dropping a tear or two – this is
  In the best heroic tradition. Ajax cried, Ulysses,
  Hector. To die, I suppose, is little enough,
  Even to die in the hot morning of youth.
  But never again to see the one we love –
  That's horrible – And the horrible bare truth
  Is that I never – we never – you –

    CHRISTIAN *looks very curiously at him.* CYRANO *is saved*
    from further embarrassment by a noise of trundling wheels,
    off, the cry of the SENTRY.

SENTRY.   Look at that!
CARBON (*rushing up to the parapet*).
  What is it?
SENTRY (*incredulous*).
          A coach and horses!

    The CADETS *rush up to see.*

CADETS.   What?
  Here in the camp? It's coming from the enemy lines.
  Fire on it! No, the coachman's making signs.
  He's shouting something. On His Majesty's
  Service. Impossible. No. Can't you hear it? His
  Majesty's Service –
DE GUICHE (*amazed*). What, the King?
CARBON.   Fall in!
DE GUICHE. Hats off, in line, come on, you ragged lot.
  A royal reception.
CARBON.   Drums at the ready! Begin!

> The CADETS *are lined up, the drums roll. Uncovered, all*
> *stand like ramrods. Onto the stage comes a coach, with*
> *driver and tigers.*

DE GUICHE. Lower the step. Open the door.

> LE BRET *obeys. The door opens and discloses* ROXANE,
> *fresh, smart, smiling.*

ROXANE.   Good
  morning.
DE GUICHE (*gaping*).
  You – the King's service.
ROXANE.   The one and only king –
  Love.
CYRANO (*overcome with the madness of it*).
        Oh God in heaven.
CHRISTIAN (*tottering*).   You – here – but why?
ROXANE. This siege of yours has lasted too long.
CYRANO.   I
  Daren't look at her.
DE GUICHE.   You can't stay here.
ROXANE.   Why not?
  Give me a drum to sit on.

⌈*One is brought. She sits, gay, beautiful, breathing Parisian*
⌊*chic.*

Thank you. What
A journey it's been. A patrol very rudely shot
At my coach. It looks, doesn't it, as though
It's been magicked out of a pumpkin – you know –
Cinderella – Good morning again. Why so sad,
All of you? Do you know, it's quite a way
From Arras. Cyrano, I'm terribly glad
To see you.

CYRANO.   Roxane. You'd better tell us how –

ROXANE. I found your army? I can't tell it now
Too long a story. But what horrors. Grey
And murky battlefields, corpses and casualties –
If *that's* your king's service, mine's better than his.

CYRANO. But this is madness. How did you get through?

ROXANE. Easy, really. All we had to do
Was trot along. If some hidalgo or don
Thrust in his head to know what was going on,
I put on my best smile. And – please, I don't mean
To disparage the French – but, really, I've never seen
Such courtesy, such gallantry. Bowing low,
Or throwing a salute, they let us go.

CARBON. Didn't they ask you where you were going?

ROXANE.   Often.
And when I told them – well, the news would soften
Their ferocity even more. All I had to say
When we were challenged was 'I'm on my way
To see my lover.' They couldn't have been sweeter.
They bowed and murmured: '*Vaya, señorita.*'

CHRISTIAN. But Roxane –

ROXANE.   I know. 'Husband' is what I
   should

Have said, of course. But that would have done no
  good.

CHRISTIAN. You don't seem to–

ROXANE.   What's the matter?

DE GUICHE.   Madame, you
  Cannot stay here.

CYRANO.   You must go away.

LE BRET. Quickly too.

CHRISTIAN.   You must.

DE GUICHE.   At once.

ROXANE (*pouting*).   Christian, do
  You want me to go?

CYRANO.   There's the small matter of
  A battle.

ROXANE.   Have your battle. I stay with my love,
  My husband. If he dies, we die together.

DE GUICHE. This sector of the line – it's doubtful whether
  Anyone can survive –

CYRANO (*grimly*).   And that is why
  He put *us* here.

ROXANE.   I see. You want me to be
  A widow?

DE GUICHE.   I swear I had no such –

ROXANE.   I swear I
  Am staying here. Call it a temporary
  Madness. Besides, it's a – new experience.

CYRANO.   So
  The future chronicles of France can show
  A *précieuse* could be heroic?

ROXANE (*hurt*).   Cyrano,
  Remember I'm your cousin.

FIRST CADET.   We'll defend you.

ROXANE. Thank you. I never doubted that, my friend.

SECOND CADET.   You
  Can smell perfume all over the camp.

He totters. It may be because of hunger.

ROXANE (*preening herself in a mirror*). I bought
This hat specially for the battle. Isn't it time,
Monsieur le Comte, you got it ready?
DE GUICHE. I'm
Going to inspect my cannon. I'd never have thought
It possible – There's time to change your –
ROXANE. I stay.
DE GUICHE. I'm going.

Shaking his head at this female obstinacy, he does so.

FIRST CADET. She stays.
CADETS (*severally*). Lend me your comb. Please may
I borrow that brush? This tunic's a disgrace.
ROXANE (*to* CARBON).
No! Nothing is going to make me budge from this
place,
His place.
CARBON (*having sighed deeply*).
Very well. Let me present
My friends and comrades – gentlemen whose intent
Is to die bravely – here – before your face.
Baron de Peyrescous de Colignac –
FIRST CADET. Madame.
CARBON. Baron de Casterac de Cahuzac. Vidame
De Magouyre Estressac Lébas d'Escarabiot.
Chevalier d'Antignac-Juzet. Baron Hollot
De Blaganc-Saléchan de Castel-Crabioules.
ROXANE. So many names!
FIRST CADET. They're all we have.
CARBON. If you'll
Be good enough to open your hand –

ROXANE does so and lets fall her handkerchief. CARBON
picks it up.

ROXANE.   But why?
CARBON. We lost the company flag. This will fly high
  Shedding perfume over the camp in its place.
ROXANE. It's very small.
CARBON.   Yes, but it's genuine lace.

> *The handkerchief is affixed to a pike and set on the parapet
> during the following.*

FIRST CADET. I could die happy now, if only I'd
  Even a walnut climbing down inside.
CARBON. Ignoble – to talk of food in the presence of
  So exquisite a lady.
ROXANE.   But I'd love
  Some breakfast – a little pâté, a cold bird,
  Wine. Would you be good enough – ? Absurd,
  You think? It's all there in my coach.
FIRST CADET.   What?
SECOND CADET.   *What?*
ROXANE. Partridges, pheasants, *crème brûlée* – the lot.
  But it has to be carved and served, the sauce reheated
  If you wish. Look at that man there, seated
  On the coachman's box. You recognize him? A very
  Precious man.

> *The coachman pulls off his hat and muffler and reveals
> himself. The* CADETS *hail him with joy.*

CADETS.   Ragueneau!
ROXANE.   Poor boys.
CYRANO (*kissing her hand*).   Our good fairy.
RAGUENEAU. Gentlemen –
CADETS.   Bravo!
RAGUENEAU.   The Spaniards let it
      through –
  The wine, the poultry, and the pastry too.

He unloads the coach, with the assistance of the two tigers
and the CADETS. CYRANO *has something more urgent than*
food to attend to. He tries to get CHRISTIAN *to himself, with*
no success.

CYRANO. Christian –

RAGUENEAU.   Distracted by their gallantry,
They missed the galantine.

CYRANO.   A word with you.

RAGUENEAU. These cushions here are stuffed with pigeons
– see!
Preoccupied with Venus's face and grace,
They missed these trophies of Diana's chase.

CYRANO (*urgently*).
We have to talk –

ROXANE.   Spread the board. Christian,
Make yourself useful.

To a sprightly tune from BERTRANDOU's *flute and the*
spanking of a drum, the victuals are spread downstage. The
CADETS *leap on to the cold fowls and gorge.* ROXANE
supervises.

SIXTH CADET.   Well, at least we scoff
Before the blasted bullets see us off.
Give me a drumstick for this blasted drum.

Meaning a chicken leg for his hollow stomach. He sees
ROXANE *come near and changes his coarse language for*
something more courtly.

Delicious – a celestial viaticum.

RAGUENEAU (*bringing out wine*).
Flagons of rubies, jars of potable gold.

ROXANE (*to* CHRISTIAN).
Quick, where's the cutlery?

RAGUENEAU.   These lanterns hold
More precious stuff than light.

*He detaches the coach lamps and starts pouring from them
into glasses held by the cadets.*

CYRANO (*grabbing* CHRISTIAN).

                                                We have to talk.
RAGUENEAU. The handle of my whip – is all pure pork.

*He strips off its integument and discloses a long sausage.
This is seized, broken, munched.*

ROXANE. Even if the rest of the army has to starve,
  At least the Gascons have a joint to carve –
  Before – we're – carved.

*There is an instant's cessation of eating at her words. But it
is soon resumed.*

                              And if de Guiche arrives –
FIRST CADET. Nothing for him.

                              Come, now, forks, spoons,
    knives,
Plates.
(*To a gorging* CADET) Plenty of time. Drink this.

She gives him a full glass.

                                              You should
  Chew, not gulp. You're *crying?*
FIRST CADET (*sobbing and eating*).   It's too good.
ROXANE (*an energetic hostess*).
    Come – white or red? Bread for Monsieur Le Bret.
    A little pastry? Toast and duck pâté?
    Vin de Bourgogne. Chicken. Try a wing.
    Christian?
CHRISTIAN (*serving out*).
              Thank you. I couldn't eat a thing.
  Why did you come?

LE BRET (*eating, but also keeping watch*).
                    De Guiche!
                              I'll tell you soon.
CYRANO. Stow everything. Knives, forks, plates, that
    spoon –

Meaning one that a CADET, *busy with a whole fowl, has
tucked behind his ear.*

Bones, crumbs, the lot. Ragueneau, get up there.
Everything hidden? Fine.

The stowing of the victuals is done with astonishing speed.
DE GUICHE *enters, sniffing.*

DE GUICHE.   Something smells good. W
    You – you've changed colour
FIRST CADET.   It's this bracing air.
DE GUICHE. And *you* look cheerful.
SECOND CADET.   So a soldier should
    When the enemy's on his way.
DE GUICHE.   Captain, you too
    Look unnaturally healthy.
CARBON.   Oh?
DE GUICHE (*to* ROXANE).
                         And as for you,
    Have you changed your mind?
ROXANE (*emphatically*).   No.
DE GUICHE (*forcefully*).   Go while you can.
ROXANE. No.
DE GUICHE (*sighing*).
                    Very well, then. Give me a musket. I
    Am staying too.
CYRANO.   Spoken, sir, like a man.
    At last you're showing Gascon fortitude.
DE GUICHE. I don't desert ladies in danger.

FIRST CADET.   Why
 Don't we give him something?

 Something formerly held in suspension in his mouth he now
 openly chews.

DE GUICHE.   You mean food?
SIXTH CADET (*somewhat drunk*).
 Food in all its multiple manifestations.
DE GUICHE (*with great scorn*).
 Do you think I'd eat your leavings?
CYRANO.   Congratulations.
 You're making progress.
DE GUICHE.   I fight, sir, and I fast.
 This condemned man requires no breakfast, not –
 Pocapdedious – like this motherless brood.
CYRANO. Hear that – *Pocapdedious*? It seems we've got
 A new recruit. He's one of us at last.

 The CADETS *cheer, some of them ironically.* CARBON *comes*
 up.

CARBON. My pikemen are lined up – accoutred, armed.
DE GUICHE (*to* ROXANE).
 Madame, will you inspect them with me?
ROXANE.   Charmed.

 He offers his arm, which she takes. They go off together.
 CYRANO *leads* CHRISTIAN *downstage.*

CHRISTIAN. Something to say, you say?
CYRANO.   Important.
CHRISTIAN.   You'd
 better
 Speak quickly.

PIKEMEN (*off*). Vivat! Vivat!
CYRANO.   Listen –

CHRISTIAN.   What?

CYRANO. Roxane is going to speak not of a letter –
   But of letters.

CHRISTIAN.   Well?

CYRANO.   Not just a few. A lot
   The time has come to open what was hid.
   You wrote a great deal more than you thought you did.

CHRISTIAN. *What?*

CYRANO.   Look at it this way. I had the task
   Of articulating for you. I didn't ask
   Whether I should write or not. I wrote
   Without mentioning it. When I assume a commission I
      devote
   A sort of silent attention –

CHRISTIAN.   But in God's name, how?
   We're under siege, we're cut off totally.

CYRANO. Well – before dawn – it's easy enough, you see.
   I'm able to cross the lines.

CHRISTIAN (*on whom a great truth is beginning to dawn*).
                              So. I see it now.
   I've written more than I thought. To be precise,
   How many times? Once a week, say? Twice?
   Three times? Four?

CYRANO.   Rather more.

CHRISTIAN.   Every day?

CYRANO (*with some shame*).
   Yes. Every day. Twice.

CHRISTIAN.   I see. They say
   There's only one thing that will make a man
   Mad enough to –

   ROXANE *is coming, alone, from the parapet.*

CYRANO.   Quiet. She's coming.

   CHRISTIAN *greets her in great perturbation of mind.*
   CYRANO *leaves.*

CHRISTIAN.   Roxane.
ROXANE. And now at last, dear Christian –
CHRISTIAN.   Now at last
    You can tell me why you risked –
ROXANE.   At last I can.
    Blame your letters, if I can speak of blame.
    That lyric flood from the battlefield. Not a day has
        passed
    Without their burning up my day – a flame
    That blinded me at last to danger –
CHRISTIAN.   So,
    Just for a bundle of love letters –
ROXANE.   Oh no!
    You don't know your own genius. Oh, it's true
    There once was an evening of jasmine, lilac, rose,
    When I began to adore you. Your soul arose
    In perfume to my window, the true you
    Made itself known in a voice, but then that voice
    Sang to me every day. I had no choice
    But to come running. If patient Penelope
    Had received such letters from her lord Ulysses,
    She would not have woven woven endlessly
    But rushed to him to cover him with kisses,
    Maddened with love as Helen once was maddened.
CHRISTIAN. But –
ROXANE.   I read your letters, reread, re-reread
        them,
    Saddened by my unworthiness, but gladdened
    By the knowledge that you, like Jupiter,
    Had descended to me, a hapless Semele,
    Your words all golden petals. The flower that shed them
    Your soul, a soul afire with sincerity.
CHRISTIAN. The sincerity – that came across then?
ROXANE.   Oh,
    My cross is the cross of my stupidity.

My soul sinks to its knees, from which, I know,
Your love will raise me. But the heart that lies
Crushed by love's burden cannot be raised. It cries:
'Forgive me, dearest. Let me veil my eyes
In anguish. Tell me how I can atone
For the sin that lies upon me like a stone –
The insult of loving you for your beauty alone.'

CHRISTIAN (*desperately perturbed*).
Heavens!

ROXANE.   Later I learned, just as a bird
Learns how to soar, to feel my spirit stirred
By the totality of you, flesh and soul,
Loving the two together. But the goal
Of true love should be elsewhere –

CHRISTIAN (*frightened*).   What do you
Love now?

ROXANE (*ecstatically*).
                You, the essential you, the true
Free being hidden by the casual dress
Of flesh I loved you for at first. I can guess
What torture it was for a great soul like yours
To see love lavished on mere caricatures
Of your true self – the eyes, the lips, the hair –
But then, with wisdom, with most patient care,
You showed me that in words, *your* words, the key
Lay that would lay bare your heart. I see
That first fair specious image now no more.

CHRISTIAN (*muttering*).
I don't like this one bit –

ROXANE.   What I loved before
Was a mere bauble. Now I love a soul.

CHRISTIAN. I'd rather be loved as people usually are –
With a bit of body as well –

ROXANE.   Here, then, the crux:
Henceforth I shall find distraction in your looks.

Your beauty is a barrier to you.
If you were ugly, twisted all askew,
Dwarfish, deformed, I feel, I *know* I should
Be able to love you more. The greater good
Needs not the lesser good.

CHRISTIAN (*wretchedly*).   It was good enough
Before.

ROXANE. Tear off your beauty with a rough
Rude hand, learn an unwonted ugliness
And see how my love shines –

CHRISTIAN.   Ugly?

ROXANE.   Ah yes,
I swear it, ugly.

> CHRISTIAN *turns his back on her, faced with a terrible decision.*

CHRISTIAN.   Leave me.

ROXANE (*astonished*).   Leave you?

CHRISTIAN.   Just
For a moment. I've some thinking to do. And you must
Warm my friends – with a smile – before they –

ROXANE. Dear Christian, dear dear Christian –

> *And she goes up to the parapet to converse with the* CADETS, *who are getting their muskets ready.* CYRANO, *seeing she has gone, looks out of his tent.* CHRISTIAN *speaks to him.* CYRANO *comes on.*

CHRISTIAN.   And so I
Know where I stand. You heard?

> CYRANO *nods.*

                                        She doesn't love
Me any more.

CYRANO.   Stop that, Christian.

CHRISTIAN.   It's *you.*

She loves my soul. You are my soul.

CYRANO.   Too true.

CHRISTIAN. And you love her.

CYRANO.   I?

CHRISTIAN.   I know.

CYRANO (*quietly, after a pause*).   That too
Is true

CHRISTIAN. Madly.

CYRANO.   More.

CHRISTIAN.   Tell her.

CYRANO.   No.

CHRISTIAN.   Why not?

CYRANO. Look at me!

CHRISTIAN.   Oh yes, ugly. Ugliness is what
She wants. She wants me to be ugly.

CYRANO.   Yes.
I heard. Can you blame me if I bless the thought?
But *you* mustn't believe it, you must not
Believe she wishes you to –

CHRISTIAN (*emphatically*).   Let her choose.
Tell her everything.

CYRANO.   Not this cross, this gallows –

CHRISTIAN. Cyrano, look at me. I'm a nonentity
Cursed with a pretty face. Must I destroy
Your happiness for that?

CYRANO.   And this mere trickery
Of words I have, because of that –

CHRISTIAN.   Go back
With her. Love her. You deserve it. Joy,
You deserve it. God, I'm on the rack
With being my own rival. I want to be –

CYRANO.   Come –

CHRISTIAN. Loved for what I am, comely and dumb,
Or else not loved at all. Can't you see,
Clever as you are, that basic simplicity?

As for our marriage – that was a fraud –
Clandestine – unrecorded – and, dear Lord,
Unconsummated. Two beds. Both cold.

CYRANO. Get thee behind me. It will hold
Till doomsday. After. This whole discussion is
Academic. We're both going to die.

CHRISTIAN. No! You must live. As for dying, that's my
Duty now.

CYRANO. You're being obstinate.

CHRISTIAN. For what I
Am, or not at all. I'm going to see
What's happening there. Talk to her. Let her
Choose.

CYRANO. I know what her choice will be –
You.

CHRISTIAN. I suppose I can hope. Roxane!

CYRANO. No, no.

ROXANE (*coming down*).
What is it?

CHRISTIAN. Cyrano has something to say –
Important.

He goes up to the parapet and takes his musket.

ROXANE. Important? Oh, he's gone.
I seem to have said something to upset him.

CYRANO. I know what you said. Did you mean what you
said?
Don't be afraid of saying it to me.
Even if he were ugly?

ROXANE. Even if he –

Gunfire begins. The CADETS *go into battle, including*
CHRISTIAN.

CYRANO. Ah, they've started. Terribly ugly?

ROXANE. Terribly.

CYRANO. Twisted? Deformed? Grotesque?
ROXANE. How could he be
Anything but noble, sublime, great-souled?
CYRANO. You'd still
Love him?
ROXANE. All the more.
CYRANO. God, is it possible
After all? Possible? Roxane, listen to me.

But LE BRET *rushes on and up to* CYRANO. *He whispers something.*

CYRANO. No.
ROXANE. What? What's happening?
CYRANO. I can never
Say it now. Finished.
ROXANE. You were going to
Tell me something.
CYRANO. Something. Yes. Whatever
It was doesn't matter now. Here's something new
To tell you. Christian – this I swear because
It's God's own truth – was a great soul.
ROXANE (*agitated*). Was?
You say *was*? Aaaaah –
CYRANO. It's over.

CADETS *bring in the dying* CHRISTIAN *and lay him gently down.* ROXANE *runs to him.*

ROXANE. Christian!
LE BRET. He
Was first over the parapet. The first shot
Got him.
CARBON. They're attacking! Come on – steady –
Muskets! Cannon!
ROXANE. Christian!

CYRANO *speaks quietly to* CHRISTIAN *while* ROXANE *sobs.*

CYRANO.   I told her everything.
It's you she loves.
CHRISTIAN.   Roxane!
CARBON. Measure your fireline! Fire! Bayonets ready!

We hear the shattering noise of the guns.

ROXANE. Speak, my love –
CARBON.   Charge!
ROXANE.   He's not dead? Speak,
My love, my love. I feel his cheek
Cold against mine – A letter here – for me.

She takes the letter from CHRISTIAN's *bosom.*

CYRANO. My letter – Roxane, I must go. They need me,
see.
ROXANE. Stay awhile. He's dead. You were his friend,
The only one to know his greatness.
CYRANO.   Yes,
Roxane.
ROXANE. He was a great soul, wasn't he?
CYRANO. Yes, Roxane.
ROXANE.   Genius, nobility, no end
To his magnificence of spirit. Purity,
Such depth of heart, such tenderness.
CYRANO. Yes, Roxane.
ROXANE.   And now – and now – gone.

She weeps bitterly.

CYRANO. And I must die today, knowing that she,
Unknowing, weeps for him but mourns for me.
DE GUICHE (*off*).
The signal! Reinforcements coming! Hang on!
ROXANE. On this letter – his blood – his tears –
VOICE.   Surrender!
CADETS. No!

ROXANE. His – brave blood. His – tender –
Tears –

> *She faints.* RAGUENEAU, *who has been cowering under the coach, runs to her. The tigers have made themselves scarce.*

RAGUENEAU.
This battle – suicide –
CYRANO. Get her away.
I'm going to lead the charge.

> DE GUICHE *staggers on, with an arm wound.*

You've proved your
Valour, monsieur. Now do what you have to do –
Get her away.
DE GUICHE. I'll get her away. If you
Can hang on here awhile, we'll win.

> ROXANE *comes to. She staggers off with* DE GUICHE *and* RAGUENEAU.

CYRANO. We'll see.
Goodbye, Roxane.

> CARBON *totters on, wounded.*

CARBON. We're falling back. I got two
Hits in the shoulder –
CYRANO (*calling encouragement*).
Reculez pas! Hardi!
Drollos! Don't worry. I
Have two deaths to avenge – Christian – my
Happiness.

> *He raises the pike with Roxane's handkerchief on it.*

And so fly high,
Little flag. *Tombé dessus! Escrasas tous!*
Pipe, piper.

BERTRANDOU *bravely shrills on his flute.*

FIRST CADET.   They're coming over!
CYRANO.   Let them. Fire!
   Fire! Fire! Charge!

   *The banner of Imperial Spain appears over the parapet. A
   Spanish officer appears.*

SPANISH OFFICER.   Who
   Are these men so anxious to be killed?
CYRANO (*firing on him*).
                   These are the Gascony cadets,
                   Captain Castel-Jaloux's their chief –
                   Barons who scorn mere baronets –
                   These are the Gascony cadets –

   The rest is lost in the noise of battle.
                              CURTAIN

Act V

A convent garden

*It is fifteen years later – 1655. The large garden of the Convent
of the Ladies of the Cross in Paris is rich in autumn foliage. A
flight of stone steps leads up to the gate. In the centre of the stage
is a great tree set in the centre of a small oval space. To the left is
the conventual house. To the right, a stone bench. Up right, a
chapel. In front of the bench there is a sewing frame, beside it a
small chair. In a basket there are skeins of silk and wool. The
tapestry in the frame is unfinished.* NUNS *are coming and going
across the garden. Some seat themselves on the bench with*
MOTHER MARGUÉRITE DE JÉSUS. *Leaves fall. The* NUNS *sing an
autumn carol.*

NUNS.   Around comes the autumn,
             The swallows are leaving,
             The year is unweaving
             Its garment of red.
             Out of his hiding
             The winter is riding,
             So Nature lies still
             And pretends to be dead.
             Aspen and yew
             Will be quivering and bare.
             What will we do?

We'll be shivering the air
With a round
Will come Christmas,
The feast of the stranger,
The beasts in the manger
Will fall on their knees.
Green in the cloister
And green on the altar,
A promise that green
Will return to the trees.

SISTER MARTHE, *who first speaks, was formerly the duenna of Roxane.*

SISTER MARTHE. Sister Claire admired her new coif in the
mirror.
Twice.

MOTHER MARGUÉRITE. Less a sin than an aesthetic error.
Very plain.

SISTER CLAIRE. That's one tale. Here's another.
Sister Marthe is a thief, Reverend Mother.
She stole a plum from the plum pie when the cook
Had her back turned.

SISTER MARTHE.   It was a very small plum.

SISTER CLAIRE. My look in the mirror was a very small
look.

SISTER MARTHE. Two looks.

SISTER MARGUÉRITE. Monsieur de Bergerac's due to come.
This evening. It will grieve him to hear of your sins.

SISTER MARTHE. Please don't do that. You know he'll make
fun of us.

SISTER CLAIRE. He'll say that nuns are greedy.

SISTER MARTHE.   Frivolous.

MOTHER MARGUÉRITE (*smiling*).
Also good. However sternly he begins,
He always ends by saying nuns are good.
Good.

SISTER CLAIRE. It must be ten or a dozen
Years since he started his Saturday visits.
MOTHER MARGUÉRITE. More.
He's been visiting us ever since his cousin
Came here to live. Fifteen years since that sore
Sad loss of hers. She brought her widow's weeds –
As he puts it – to offset our virgin lilies.
He's very poetical. A black dove,
He once said, among grounded seagulls.
SISTER CLAIRE. His skill is
All in worldly things. Was he ever in love,
I wonder? Such a gentleman, yet he leads
A very aggressive life. Once he said to me
That there's a kind of panache in virgin vows.
What did he mean?
MOTHER MARGUÉRITE. The white plume of celibacy.
He made a rhyme about it.
SISTER MARTHE. He was always witty.
He's the only one who can make her smile.
MOTHER MARGUÉRITE. Very droll.
He likes our cake too.
SISTER CLAIRE. It's such a pity
He's not a good Catholic.
SISTER MARTHE. We'll convert him in time.
MOTHER MARGUÉRITE (*severely*).
No, I forbid you to meddle with his soul.
He may stop coming here.
SISTER MARTHE. But how about God?
MOTHER MARGUÉRITE. Rest easy. God, being omniscient,
Knows all about Monsieur de Bergerac.
SISTER MARTHE. There's not one Saturday I haven't heard
him say:
'Ah, dear sister –' And in a proud sort of way,
Too. 'Dear sister – I ate meat yesterday.'
MOTHER MARGUÉRITE. Really? I'd be more ready for praise
than blame

If he was telling the truth. The last time he came,
He hadn't eaten for three days.
SISTER CLAIRE.   Oh, no.
MOTHER MARGUÉRITE. He's poor, very poor.
SISTER MARTHE.   Who told you
    so?
MOTHER MARGUÉRITE. Monsieur Le Bret.
SISTER CLAIRE.   Apart from
    things like prayer,
Why doesn't somebody help him?
MOTHER MARGUÉRITE.   Nobody dare.

> *Upstage, on a tree-lined path,* ROXANE *can be seen, widow-capped, long-veiled.* DE GUICHE, *grown magnificently old, is with her. They walk slowly.* MOTHER MARGUÉRITE *rises.*

We'd better go in. She has a visitor.
SISTER MARTHE.
The Duc de Grammont, as he is now.
SISTER CLAIRE.   The Marshal, is it?
SISTER MARTHE. A long time since he came to call on her.
SISTER CLAIRE. He's busy, I suppose. The court—the camp—
    The world—

> *She shudders at that last word. The* NUNS *go in.* ROXANE *and* DE GUICHE *come down in silence, stopping near the embroidery frame.*

DE GUICHE.   A long time. Too long. God knows
How you can bring yourself to cheat men's eyes
Of all that golden beauty. You propose
To stay here for ever, in mourning?
ROXANE.   For ever.
DE GUICHE.   Ever
    Faithful?
ROXANE. Faithful. My future lies

Among the faithful.
DE GUICHE.   Have you forgiven me?
ROXANE.   I'm here. That has to mean I've forgiven you.
DE GUICHE.   Christian – was he really so – ?
ROXANE.   If you knew
     him.
DE GUICHE.   I didn't know him. I didn't particularly
     Want to know him. That last letter of his –
     Do you still wear it next to your –
ROXANE.   Still and for ever.
     Like a sacred relic.
DE GUICHE.   I'll never understand
     Such a sterile devotion.
ROXANE.   But to me
     He isn't really dead. It's as if we
     Still meet in some special region, sustained
     Only by love – not devotion – living love,
     Love between the living.
DE GUICHE.   Do you see much of
     The other man?
ROXANE (*lighting up*).
                      Cyrano? Oh yes, he pays
     A weekly visit, acts as my gazette,
     My court circular, out on Saturdays.
     Under that tree, if the weather's fine, they set
     A chair for him. I wait with my embroidery.
     At four o'clock the clock strikes,
     And on the last stroke I hear his step
     And his stick tapping the stone steps. He's so
     Regular, I never turn to see.
     First, he laughs at me for what he likes
     To call my Penelope web, and, after, he
     Retails the chronicle of the week, and –

     LE BRET, *ageing, in an old coat, appears, unhappy.*

There's Le Bret.

Le Bret, how's our friend?

LE BRET.   Not well, not well at all.

ROXANE (*to* DE GUICHE).

He's exaggerating.

LE BRET.   It's just as I say,
  Just as I've always said – loneliness,
  Wretchedness. He writes those satires of his,
  Determined to make more and more enemies.
  He attacks false saints, false nobles, false heroes,
  Plagiaristic poets – in fact, more or less
  Everyone. That's no life for anyone.

ROXANE.   Everyone goes
  In terror of that sword of his, that's one thing.
  No one dares touch him.

DE GUICHE (*doubtfully*).   That may be so.

LE BRET. Oh, it isn't the violence I fear – it's this loneliness,
  As I said. It's hunger, poverty, ravening
  December with wolves at its heels battering
  The door of his dark hovel. Soon they'll catch
  Our swordsman off his guard. Every day, you know,
  He has to tighten his belt by one more notch.
  Even his poor old nose isn't the same –
  It's like discoloured ivory. And he has only
  One rusty, rotting black serge coat to his name.

DE GUICHE (*with referred stoicism*).
  This is the world. This is how the world goes.
  He takes what comes. Don't pity him too much.

LE BRET (*smiling bitterly*).
  My lord marshal –

DE GUICHE (*firmly*).   Don't pity him, I say. He
  Lives his life as he wants, he's one of those
  Rare animals that have opted to be free.

LE BRET. My lord duke –

DE GUICHE.   I know. I have everything. And

He has nothing, save that one thing. Nevertheless,
I think I'd be proud to shake him by the hand.
Now I have to go.

ROXANE.   I'll go with you
As far as the gate.

> DE GUICHE *salutes* LE BRET *and turns with* ROXANE *towards the steps. They start to climb it. Then he turns to* LE BRET.

DE GUICHE.   I think I envy him, yes,
Envy him. There's such a thing as success
Which sickens like excess. When a man wins
The big prizes – having no glaring sins
To reproach himself with, filling the foreground up –
He feels sinful nevertheless, defiled from top
To toe – not with remorse, remorse is too
Considerable a thing – rather as though
Under the silk, under the velvet and ermine,
There crawled a vague disquieting breed of vermin
Unknown to moral entomologists.
Pride bloats to more pride; power never rests.
The ducal robe sweeps up the endless stair
With a dry rustle of dead illusions, a sere
Whistle of regrets. Just as your veil there,
Trailing as you mount this literal stair,
Draws a whisper of dead leaves along.

ROXANE.   I must say
The sentiment does you honour.

DE GUICHE.   Yes? Le Bret!
(*To* ROXANE)
Permit us – a brief word.

> He goes down to LE BRET *and speaks quietly.*

                    It's true. No one
Dares to attack your friend, not openly.
But the hate grows, and hate will find its way.

I think you ought to warn him. The other day
At court, one of his haters said to me:
'De Bergerac may die – accidentally.'
LE BRET. I see.
DE GUICHE.   I hope you see. Tell him to stay
  At home. To be careful.
LE BRET.   Careful! Whatever I say,
  He treads his own path. He's coming here today.
  All right, I'll warn him, but –
ROXANE (*on the step, to a* NUN *who approaches her*).
                            Yes, what is it?
NUN. This man Ragueneau would like a word with you,
  Madame.
ROXANE.   Very well. Bring him to me.
  (*To* DE GUICHE *and* LE BRET)
                                    I suppose
  He's come for sympathy – something to warm him on
  His long cold downward road. The things he's done –
  Pastrycook, poet, singer –
LE BRET.   Bathhouse attendant –
ROXANE. Actor –
LE BRET.   Parish beadle –
ROXANE.   Hairdresser –
LE BRET.   Teacher of
  guitar.
ROXANE. Poor man – his fortunes always in the
  descendant.
  What next, I wonder.

      RAGUENEAU *comes in hurriedly, agitated. His fatness is
      clothed in miserable grey.*

RAGUENEAU.   Dear madame. Your grace.
ROXANE (*smiling*).
  First tell your troubles, if troubles they are,
  To Monsieur Le Bret.

RAGUENEAU. But madame—

ROXANE's *smile forbids further speech. She mounts the stair with* DE GUICHE. RAGUENEAU *comes down to* LE BRET.

I suppose, after all — I mean — in any case,
It's not the sort of thing that — not yet,
Anyhow —

LE BRET. What, man?

RAGUENEAU. I went to see him just now,
Our friend, I mean — he was just coming out
Of his lodgings. I hurried on to meet him, but
He was walking quickly. At the corner of the street
There's this upper window — he was passing under it —
I wonder if it could really have been
An accident — I wonder — anyway, oh my God,
A servant, a big hairy lout, he let
A chunk of wood drop, a great heavy log fall,
Fall—

LE BRET.
On top of — oh no —

RAGUENEAU. A massive chunk of wood.

LE BRET. What are you trying to tell me?

RAGUENEAU. He was lying
there.
I ran up to him as quickly as I could.
A great gash in his —

LE BRET. Dead?

RAGUENEAU. Just about alive.
I carried him up to his room. Have you seen it? I've
Never seen such — squalor. Oh, my God.

LE BRET. Is he suffering?

RAGUENEAU. I don't think so. I don't think he feels
Anything.

LE BRET. Did you get a —

RAGUENEAU. A doctor came, yes, out of
charity.

LE BRET. God help him. We mustn't tell her. She
   Mustn't know, not yet. What did he say,
   This doctor – what did he – ?
RAGUENEAU.   Technicalities –
   Meningeal fever. Lesion of the
   Something or other. Oh, if you'd seen him,
   Lying there – blood – bandages –
   But you will now, of course, right away.
   We must go quickly. He's all by himself there.
   If he tries to get up, and he will, I know he will –
   He may, he may –
LE BRET (*drawing him to the right*).
   Through the chapel – that's the shortest way –

   ROXANE *appears on the stairway and calls* LE BRET *as he
   and* RAGUENEAU *hurry to the chapel.*

ROXANE. Monsieur Le Bret!

   But the two go off without responding.

                         Going off when I call him?
   Ragueneau, poor man, must have been unusually
   Pathetic.

   She comes slowly down.

                 This last September day
   Makes my old sorrow smile. It's as though
   April had come to golden maturity,
   So that the fall is really the fall of spring,
   A gentle end the mirror of a gentle beginning.

   She sits down to her embroidery. SISTERS MARTHE *and*
   CLAIRE *bring an armchair and place it under the tree.*

ROXANE. The old chair, for my old friend.
SISTER MARTHE.   The best of all
   The chairs in our parlour.

ROXANE. Thank you.

They leave. She sews. The clock strikes.

So. The last stroke.
The hour. This is strange. He was
Never late before. Perhaps the nun
Who's always trying to convert him is trying again.
(*A pause*)
I've never known him to be as late as this.
He ought to be converted by now.

SISTER MARTHE (*appearing on the steps*).

Here he is,
Madame.
(*More formally*)
Monsieur de Bergerac.

ROXANE (*following her old custom of not turning her head to greet him*).

These
Old faded colours – difficult to match them.

She embroiders. CYRANO, *very pale, his hat over his eyes, appears at the top of the stairway. The nun goes away, troubled by his appearance. He comes down the steps leaning on his stick, keeping upright only by a visible effort.* ROXANE *speaks to him in friendly banter.*

ROXANE. Late for the first time, Cyrano –
After fifteen years.

CYRANO *reaches his seat with difficulty, his cheerful tone in terrible contrast to his tortured face.*

CYRANO. Forgive me, please.
I was detained, I'm afraid.

ROXANE. Well?

CYRANO. By an unexpected visitor.

ROXANE (*carelessly, working away*).

                               Was it a

  Tiresome visitor?

CYRANO.   Very tiresome.

ROXANE.   And you sent him

  away?

CYRANO. For the time being. 'This is Saturday,'
I said. 'And on Saturday I have a
Regular engagement. Do me the favour
Of returning in an hour or so.'

ROXANE. He'll have to wait some time. I shan't let you go
Before dark.

CYRANO (*gently*).

               It's just possible, I'm afraid,
I may have to go before it's dark. My apologies.

He leans back wearily in his chair. SISTER CLAIRE *appears,*
ostensibly to cut some parsley.

ROXANE. You're neglecting your duties, Cyrano. Here is
Someone waiting to be teased.

CYRANO (*opening eyes he has wearily shut*).

                       Ah, yes.

Come here, sister. You of the beautiful
Downcast eyes –

The NUN, *approaching obediently according to the comic*
tradition she has established with CYRANO, *raises those eyes*
and is shocked by CYRANO's *face.* CYRANO *urgently*
indicates that she must not betray her shock to ROXANE.

               I have something to confess.
I ate meat again yesterday. Isn't that terrible?

SISTER CLAIRE. Terrible. And as a penance you must come
To the refectory later and have a nice big bowl
Of bouillon.

CYRANO.   I'll be there.

SISTER CLAIRE.   You're becoming quite
   reasonable,
Monsieur.
ROXANE.   At last you're breaking his obstinate soul.
Now is the time to convert him.
SISTER CLAIRE.   Oh, no, no,
That's something I mustn't do.
CYRANO.   True. And something
You've never, in all these years, tried to do.
Bursting with virtue like a spiritual plum,
And yet you never preach. Astonishing.
But now, sister, I'm going to astonish *you*.
I'm going to let you pray for me.
ROXANE.   Look at her –
CYRANO. Tonight at vespers.
ROXANE.   Struck absolutely dumb.
SISTER CLAIRE. You forgot one advantage of my calling,
   Monsieur.
I can pray without permission. And I will.

She goes off, troubled. CYRANO *turns to* ROXANE, *bending
over her work.*

CYRANO. Patient Penelope is weaving still.
There's one thing everyone can be sure about
And that is that, alas, I'll never see
How that piece of work eventually turns out.
ROXANE (*smiling*).
I wondered how long it would be
Before you said that.

A flurry of wind sends some leaves down.

CYRANO.   The year unweaves
Her tapestry. Look at them.
ROXANE.   Such colour.
Perfect Venetian red. They're falling fast.

CYRANO. They fall well. With a sort of panache.
   They plume down in their last
   Loveliness, disguising their fear
   Of being dried and pounded to ash
   To mix with the common dust.
   They go in grace, making their fall appear
   Like flying.
ROXANE.   You're melancholy today.
CYRANO. Never. I'm not the melancholy sort.
ROXANE. Very well, then. We'll let
   The leaves of the fall fall while you
   Turn the leaves of my gazette.
   What's new at court?
CYRANO.   Let me see, let me see.
   Saturday the nineteenth. His Majesty
   Was ill after eating too much preserved ginger –
   Eight helpings, to be precise. The court's decree
   Was that it was high treason so to injure
   The royal viscera. So there and then
   The offending ginger was condemned to death,
   And the royal pulse slowed to normal again.
   What next? Ah yes, Sunday the twentieth.
   The Queen gave a great ball, and they burned
   Seventeen hundred and sixty-three wax candles.
   A minor item: our army, so it's learned,
   Has been victorious in Austria. There have been some
      scandals
   To do with witches. A bishop went to heaven,
   Or so it's believed: there's been as yet no report
   Of his arrival. Madame d'Athis's dog, a sort
   Of hairier smaller Madame d'Athis, was given
   An enema –
ROXANE.   Monsieur de Bergerac, that will do.
CYRANO. Monday, the twenty-first – nothing. Lygdamire
   has a new lover.

ROXANE (*indicating that this is always happening*).
>Oh.

CYRANO. Tuesday, the twenty-second,
The entire court removed to Fontainebleau.
Wednesday: the Comte de Fiesque unequivocally
  beckoned
To Madame de Montglat. It's believed that she said no.
Thursday, La Mancini was Queen of France,
Or very nearly. Friday, during a dance,
Madame de Montglat, so the rumours go,
Said yes. Saturday, the twenty-sixth –

He closes his eyes. His head falls. Silence. ROXANE, *surprised, turns, looks, is frightened, rises, goes towards him.*

ROXANE. Cyrano!
CYRANO (*opening his eyes*).
>Yes? What? What is it?

He sees ROXANE *bending over him. He quickly pulls down his hat over his face, leaning away from her.*

>It's nothing,
Nothing at all. I shall be all right. Just
My old wound from Arras. It likes to sting
Sometimes, to remind me that it's still there.
ROXANE. My poor dear friend.
CYRANO. It doesn't last.
It will go soon. There – it's gone.

He forces a smile.

ROXANE (*standing near him*). We all of us
Have our old wounds. Mine is here – on yellowing
Paper, bloodstained, tearstained, hardly legible.
CYRANO. His letter. Didn't you say that, one day,
You'd let me read it?

Twilight begins to fall.

ROXANE.   You want to? You really
  Want to?
CYRANO.   Yes. Today. Now.
ROXANE.   Take it, then.

She gives him the little bag from around her neck.

CYRANO. I may open it?
ROXANE.   Open it. Read it.

*She goes back to her embroidery, folding it, arranging the
silk. But* CYRANO *does not open the letter.*

CYRANO.   'Goodbye,
  Roxane. For this is the last time I
  Shall be able to write –'
ROXANE (*surprised*).   Aloud?
CYRANO.   'I have to die
  Some time today. My beloved, how
  Heavy my heart is, and it is heavy too
  With so great a burden of love, love still untold,
  Perhaps unguessed at, unprospected gold
  From love's new world, not to be mined, for now
  The time for its shining forth is gone, all gone.
  Never more shall my eyes kiss the sight of you,
  The flight of your gestures. I think of one –
  The way you have of pushing back a strand
  Of your hair from your forehead – and
  My heart wants to cry out –'
ROXANE.   You read it,
  You read it in such a way –

The night is approaching.

CYRANO.   'But now I can only cry:
  Goodbye, my dearest –'
ROXANE.   In such a voice –
CYRANO.   'Goodbye,

My angel, my heart's treasure, my one love –'
ROXANE. A voice, I know, I am not hearing for
The first time, speaking such words –
CYRANO. 'Never for one second has my heart
Been absent from your presence. And, as the night
Deepens, the shadows of the next world start
To close in on me, I shall be that one
Whose love, raging and blessing like the sun
That outlives all men, will live on and on
Beyond the sun's limits –'
ROXANE.   How can you
Possibly read now – in this lack of light?

> *She has risen and gone to him. He opens his eyes, notices,
> makes a gesture of surprise, almost of fear, then bows his
> head. There is a long pause. Then, in a darkness still
> growing, she speaks slowly, hands clasped.*

For all of fifteen years you have played the role
Of the old friend, affectionate, droll,
But never one hint of –
CYRANO.   Roxane –
ROXANE.   So it was you.
CYRANO. Oh no, Roxane, no, no –
ROXANE.   I might
Have known, every time you spoke my name.
CYRANO. Not I, oh no –
ROXANE.   It was you.
CYRANO.   Roxane, I swear –
ROXANE. I see through it all now – that generous
Imposture – the letters – it was you.
CYRANO. No.
ROXANE.   It was always you. The mad, dear
Foolish words –
CYRANO.   No.
ROXANE.   The voice in the night,
You.

CYRANO. Upon my honour.
ROXANE.   It was all
  And always you.
CYRANO.   I never loved you.
ROXANE.   You
  Loved me.
CYRANO.   It was he who loved you.
ROXANE.   Even
  Now you love me.
CYRANO (*feebly*).   No.
ROXANE. That *no* is not so strong
  As it was a second or two ago.
CYRANO. No, no, my dear love.
  I never loved you.
ROXANE.   And all these fifteen long years,
  While you stayed silent, you knew, you knew
  That his letter was stained by *your* tears,
  Not –
CYRANO. His blood, though, stained by his blood.
ROXANE.   And
    you
  Never said, never hinted, never once. Why
  Do you break silence now?
CYRANO (*confused and weary*). Oh, because I –

  LE BRET *and* RAGUENEAU *come running in.*

LE BRET. This will be your last madness. How could you
  Be so –
  (*To* RAGUENEAU)
  He's here.
CYRANO (*smiling, trying to rise*).
              Yes indeed, I am here.
LE BRET.   You ought to know,
  Madame, that he's killed himself to come to you.
ROXANE. Oh my God, that faintness – I wondered –

CYRANO.   I

   regret
That I rudely intermitted my gazette.
On Saturday, the twenty-sixth, an hour before
Dinner, Monsieur de Bergerac
Was foully, ignobly
Murdered.

   He takes his hat off and shows the bandages swathing his head.

ROXANE (*desperately*).
               Cyrano, what have they done to you?
CYRANO. At Arras, I said I wanted to depart
With honourable steel piercing my heart
And a piercing epigram upon my lips.
That's what I said. But fate's a great buffoon,
A balloon-pricker, a deflater of the most stoic
Postures, a specialist in traps and trips.
Look at me – ambushed, taken in the rear
In a gutter for a battlefield, my heroic
Foe a scullion, his weapon a mere
Firelog. My life has played a consistent tune.
I've missed everything – even my death.
RAGUENEAU (*breaking down*).   Oh, monsieur –
CYRANO. Don't blubber, Ragueneau, my fellow poet.
Poets should be dry-eyed. Cease your sobs
And tell me what you're writing these days.

   He takes RAGUENEAU'*s hand.*

RAGUENEAU. Nothing. All I do is odd menial jobs
For Molière.
CYRANO.   Oh, Molière.
RAGUENEAU.   Yes, but I'm leaving the swine
Tomorrow. Yesterday they played *Scapin*,

His new comedy. He's stolen a whole scene
From you.
LE BRET.   That's true: the one with the great line:
'*Que diable allait-il faire en cette galère?*'
RAGUENEAU. I could murder him.
CYRANO (*evenly*).   When a poet has taste he
  can show it
By stealing from his betters. I gather his play's
A success?
RAGUENEAU. Your scene was. The audience laughed
And laughed and laughed -

  The memory makes him cry.

CYRANO (*with rancour*).   My life - all of a piece - a
  shaft
Of sun, a puff of air, and then not even
A memory. Roxane - do you recall
That night - the balcony, the ivied wall,
Christian? I stood in the shadows, underneath,
And left it to another to climb and claim
The kiss of glory. It happened again and again -
The shadow for me, for others the applause, the fame.
There's a kind of justice somewhere. Even in the teeth
Of what's to come I can say: Gentlemen,
Take down this truism in your commonplace books:
Molière has genius; Christian had good looks.

  The chapel bell is ringing. The NUNS *proceed to their
  prayers.*

They're going to pray now. Nymphs, in your orisons,
Etcetera etcetera –
ROXANE (*calling*).   Sister, sister!
CYRANO (*grasping her hand*).   No.
Don't go away. When you come back I may
Not be here.

The NUNS *have entered the chapel. An organ plays quietly.*

> A little defunctive music –
> That's all I need now.

ROXANE.　　　　　　　You must live.

> I love you.

CYRANO.　　Don't say that. That doesn't come
> Into the story. When the princess said
> *I love you* to the enchanted prince
> Who was a toad or something, all his ugliness
> Melted away under the sunlight of
> Those words. Your magic doesn't work. *Love*,
> You say. But, as you see, I'm still the same.

ROXANE.　How can I ever forgive myself? It's I
> Who have done this to you –

CYRANO (*serenely*).　　　　　Let no shred of blame
> Cling to your silk. I never had
> Much acquaintance with the
> Sweetness of woman. My mother was,
> Understandably perhaps, not pleased
> With what she'd produced. I had no
> Sister. Later, in manhood, I
> Learned to fear the
> Mistress with mockery in the tail of her eye.
> But – and God bless you for this for ever and ever –
> I have had one friend different from
> The few others.
> A friend in a silken gown in my life.

> *The moon has begun to illuminate the scene.* LE BRET *points to it.*

LE BRET.　There's another friend.

CYRANO (*smiling*).　　　　　I see her.

ROXANE (*heartbroken*).

> I never loved but one man in my life.
> Now I must lose him twice.

CYRANO. Le Bret, I shall mount soon to that opaline
   presence, plunge into that crystalline river
   Or lake of light, without a lunar machine
   Or astral rocket –
LE BRET.   What are you saying?
CYRANO.   The moon.
   There are great names up there, other friends –
   Socrates, Plato, Galileo –
LE BRET (*angrily*).   No, no!
   I won't have it. It's stupid, it's unjust.
   Such a poet, such a great
   Heart, such a man – to die like this, to die
   Like this –
CYRANO.   There he goes growling, my
   Old bear Le Bret.
LE BRET.   My dear dear dear –

   CYRANO's *delirium begins. He half rises, his eyes wan-
   dering.*

CYRANO. We are the Gascony cadets.
   Captain Castel-Jaloux – It's a matter of
   The constitution of the elementary mass.
   Yes? The *quidditas* of the *hic* – eh?
LE BRET. Delirious, all that learning –
CYRANO.   The testimony
   Of Copernicus is worth considering
   On that particular point –
ROXANE (*desperate*).   Oh no –
CYRANO. *Que diable allait-il faire en cette galère?*
   What the devil was he doing or going to do there?

   He has a moment of clarity. He declaims.

            Philosopher and scientist,
            Poet, musician, duellist,
            And voyager through space,

A sort of controversialist,
Whose wit kept to a charted track
But sped at a great pace,
A lover too, who seemed to lack
The luck in love of other men –
Here lies Hercule-Savinien
De Cyrano de Bergerac,
Nothing, everything, nothing again –
Sunk now, without trace.
I have to leave you. Sorry. I can't stay.
That lunar shaft is – waiting to carry me away,
A punctual and impatient sort of
Engine.

> *He falls back in his chair. The sobbing of* ROXANE *recalls him to reality. He looks at her. He strokes her veiled hair.*

I would not ask that you mourn any the less
That good brave Christian blessed with handsomeness,
But, when the final cold sniffs at my heart
And licks my bones, perhaps you might impart
A double sense to your long obsequies,
And make those tears, which have been wholly his,
Mine too, just a little, mine, just a –
ROXANE. My love, my only love –

> CYRANO, *shaken again by fever and delirium, brusquely raises himself. The others move forward to help him, but he brushes them away. He sets his back against the tree trunk.*

CYRANO. Not here, oh no, not lying down. Let
No one try to help me – only this
Tree. He's coming. He's coming. Already
I feel myself being shod in marble,
Gloved in lead.
(*With joy*)
        Let him come, then.

He shall find me on my feet –

He draws.

My sword in my hand.

LE BRET. Cyrano!

CYRANO. There he is, looking at me, grinning
At my nose. Who is he
To grin, that noseless one?
What's that you say – useless, useless?
You have it wrong, you empty brain pan.
You see, a man
Fights for far more than the mere
Hope of winning. Better, far better
To know that the fight is totally
Irreparably incorrigibly in vain.
A hundred against – no, a thousand.
And I recognize every one, every one of you.

He lunges at the air again and again.

All my old enemies – Falsehood, Compromise,
Prejudice, Cowardice. You ask for my
Surrender? Ah no, never, no, never. Are
You there too, Stupidity?
You above all others perhaps were predestined
To get me in the end. But no, I'll
Fight on, fight on, fight –

*He swings his sword again, then stops breathless. During
his last speech he falls into* LE BRET'*s arms.*

You take everything – the rose and the laurel too.
Take them and welcome. But, in spite of you,
There is one thing goes with me when tonight
I enter my last lodging, sweeping the bright
Stars from the blue threshold with my salute.
A thing unstained, unsullied by the brute

Broken nails of the world, by death, by doom
Unfingered – See it there, a white plume
Over the battle – A diamond in the ash
Of the ultimate combustion –

ROXANE *kisses his forehead. He opens his eyes, recognizes her, smiles.*

My panache.
CURTAIN